THE CIVILIZED
SHOPPER'S GUIDE
TO *Edinburgh*
and Glasgow

JUNE SKINNER SAWYERS

PHOTOGRAPHS BY ALEX HEWITT & SUSIE LOWE

The Little Bookroom • New York

© 2008 the Little Bookroom

Text © 2008 June Skinner Sawyers

Photographs © 2008 Alex Hewitt & Susie Lowe

Book design: Louise Fili Ltd

Library of Congress Cataloging-in-Publication Data

Sawyers, June Skinner, 1957-

The civilized shopper's guide to Edinburgh & Glasgow / by June Skinner Sawyers ;

photos by Alex Hewitt.

p. cm.

Includes indexes.

ISBN 1-892145-58-8 (alk. paper)

1. Shopping—Scotland—Edinburgh—Guidebooks.

2. Shopping—Scotland—Glasgow—Guidebooks.

3. Edinburgh (Scotland)—Guidebooks.

4. Glasgow (Scotland)—Guidebooks. I. Title.

TX337.G72E35 2008

381'.45641302411—dc22

2008009238

Published by The Little Bookroom

435 Hudson Street, 3rd floor

New York NY 10014

editorial@littlebookroom.com

www.littlebookroom.com

10 9 8 7 6 5 4 3 2 1

Printed in China

Distributed in the U.S. by Random House, in the U.K. and Ireland by

Signature Book Services, and in Europe by Random House International.

TABLE OF CONTENTS

INTRODUCTION

Wander down the streets of big cities and before long it hits you. Whether you're in New York or London, Paris or Rome, the cities of the world look more and more alike. A creeping sameness is engulfing the planet, a pall of conformity and homogeneity that threatens to destroy whatever originality remains. You see the same restaurant chains, the same franchises. It's enough to make a cynic ask, Why travel at all?

This small book is my humble attempt to answer that question. Sure, Scotland's two major cities have the same stores that you'll find in other world capitals. But they also have small, priceless independent shops along major thoroughfares and down twisting, narrow lanes. I have tried to choose a representative sample of the best, the quirkiest, the most distinctive. Some are here for historical reasons, some because of the individuality of the owner, and some because there is something about the shop—an intangible quality—that appealed to me. Most, if not all, of the shops have a strong Scottish and/or United Kingdom connection. Owners may have studied at local or regional art schools, shops may sell traditional Scottish materials (such as cashmere and tweeds), carry products that are available only in the United Kingdom, or offer items that are quintessentially British, whether "Wellie" stands or pottery designed by Scots or UK craftspeople.

Since this is also a walking guide, I have tried to be aware of the amount of time spent pounding the pavement. Hence, the shops are grouped geographically, mostly in walking order for convenience's sake. The ten walks vary considerably in the number of shops, from as few as two to more than a dozen.

I encourage you, whenever possible, to pause, look up, and take in the surrounding architecture. In Edinburgh, both the Old Town and the New Town have been classified, since 1995, as World Heritage sites. Glasgow, too, is worth noting. Although it doesn't have quite the historic charm of the capital city, it does offer some breathtaking architectural treasures. It wasn't for nothing, after all, that it was named the United Kingdom City of Architecture in 1999. Cafés and restaurants punctuate each walk. I have also included several sidebars ranging in subject from the Willow Tearooms to chocolate shops and Scottish cheeses, from farmers markets to street markets.

Enjoy and savor.

SOME PRACTICAL INFORMATION

Shopping in Scotland is similar to shopping in other parts of the UK, but there are a few things to keep in mind.

HOURS: Generally speaking, shopping hours in Scotland are Monday–Saturday from 9 or 9:30am to 5:30 or 6pm. For many years, Scotland virtually shut down on Sunday. Nowadays, though, more and more shops are staying open, especially during the annual Edinburgh Festival in August and throughout the Christmas season. Several shops close one day during the week, usually on Monday or Wednesday, while others stay open an hour late one night, usually on Thursdays. Check the opening hours of each individual shop.

BANK HOLIDAYS: "Bank holidays" is a rather antiquated phrase; legislation authorizing them dates back to 1871. Since banks were officially closed on those days, it generally was believed that no business of any sort could be conducted; hence, "bank holidays" entered into popular usage for businesses other than banks. Even so, many shops today remain open on bank holidays; it's best to check.

Holidays in Scotland differ from the rest of the UK. Scotland has nine holidays. They are as follows:

New Year's Day (*Hogmanay*)

January 2

Good Friday *(Note: Easter Monday is not an official bank holiday although it is observed by many banks and companies)*

Early May Day Bank Holiday *(first Monday in May)*
Spring Bank Holiday *(last Monday in May)*
Summer Bank Holiday *(first Monday in August)*
St. Andrew's Day *(November 30 or, if it falls on a weekend, the following Monday)*
Christmas Day
Boxing Day *(December 26)*

VAT: The government imposes a tax of roughly 19 percent on all goods purchased, which is referred to as VAT (or Valued Added Tax). That's the bad news. The good news is that non-British residents are eligible for a tax refund of about 15 percent. Just ask for a refund form from the particular retailer and request that a member of the staff fill it out.

Edinburgh

WALK 1 ✦ ROYAL MILE

CODA

12 BANK STREET / THE MOUND
☎ (0131) 622 7246 · *www.codamusic.co.uk*
MON–SAT 9:30AM–5:30PM, SUN 11AM–5PM

THE TRADITIONAL AND CONTEMPORARY FOLK MUSIC SPECIALIST CODA CARRIES THE KIND OF RECORDINGS that most general record stores simply don't stock anymore. To some, that would make it an anachronism; to others, a godsend. It's refreshing to find such quirky items as Scottish sheet music and especially the Scottish Tradition pamphlets (such as *Gaelic Psalms from Lewis* or *The Muckle Sangs: Classic Scots Ballads* published by the influential Scots record label Greentrax Recordings). Where else can you find, to cite just a few examples, *Sands of Vatersay* by the Vatersay Boys, *Mar a Tha Mo Chridhe (As My Heart Is)* by the North Uist singer and musician Julie Fowlis, or *The River Sessions* by the great Scots guitarist Bert Jansch?

Of course, the shop focuses on Scottish, Irish, and English traditional music but it also carries American artists (many with roots in the Anglo-Celtic traditions) and world music titles, as well as specific genres of music. Three listening posts at the counter allow customers to listen to a recording before purchasing it. Coda also sells traditional music magazines, DVDs, videos, and hard-to-find cassettes.

In addition, the shop serves as an informal community clearinghouse of sorts. Come here to learn what's going on in the local, regional, and national music scene, from concerts around town to the annual Celtic Connections Festival held each winter in Glasgow.

[12]

ROYAL MILE WHISKIES

379 HIGH STREET

☎ (0131) 225 3383 · *www.royalmilewhiskies.com*

MON–SAT 10AM–6PM, SUN 12:30–6PM

Although the space is small, the choice is vast—more than 400 whiskies in stock. The shop also bottles its own range under the Royal Mile Whiskies and Dormant Distillery Company labels, bottlings typically from a single cask, non-chill filtered, and bottled at cask strength.

Royal Mile Whiskies also has a strong selection of American bourbons, Canadian whiskies, blended whiskies, grain whiskies, Irish whiskies, and vatted whiskies (a mix of malt whisky from different single malt distilleries). More unusual, perhaps, is the shop's selection from Japan, including Yoichi, considered the most Scottish of Japan's distilleries. Among their selection of "world" whiskies are those from New Zealand, Australia, and India, as well as Penderyn from Wales and Mackmyra from Sweden.

Royal Mile Whiskies also sponsors regular whisky tastings: the annual Whisky Fringe is held on the second to last weekend in August (to coincide with the Edinburgh International and Fringe Festival), usually at the Mansfield Traquair, a historic church with remarkable murals by Phoebe Anna Traquair (1852-1936), located in central Edinburgh. During the event, customers can sample whiskies from around the world as well as the latest releases from a variety of distillers and bottlers, many of them rare and/or unusual drams.

At the shop, you'll also find books on whisky and whisky miniatures as well as liqueurs, meads, and wines; shortbread and biscuits; marmalades and mustards. It's a bit on the touristy side—how can it not be given its Royal Mile location?—but it's a fun place to stop and browse.

GEOFFREY (TAILOR) KILTMAKERS

57–61 HIGH STREET

☎ (0131) 557 0256

www.geoffreykilts.co.uk · www.21stcenturykilts.com

MON–SAT 9AM–5:30PM (6:30PM APR–LATE OCT)

SUN 10AM–5:30PM (6:30PM APR–LATE OCT)

A FAMILY BUSINESS SINCE 1971, GEOFFREY (TAILOR) SPECIALIZES IN GENTLEMEN'S TRADITIONAL HANDSEWN kilts made to measure in the company workshops in Edinburgh and in the West Highlands town of Oban. All traditional kilts are hand-sewn.

Geoffrey (Tailor) makes casual kilts and formal attire such as the Auld Reekie (Edinburgh's nickname), as well as ladies' kilts and children's kilts. In 1996, the company launched the 21st Century Kilts line in nontraditional fabrics (denim, leather, black and red pinstripe) in a variety of colors.

Accessories available at the shop include sporrans, ties, cummerbunds, ghillie brogues, head coverings, cufflinks, Inverness capes, buckles, kilt pins, brooches, and sgian dubhs (small daggers). For those unlucky souls whose families have no tartan or Scottish connection whatsoever, Geoffrey (Tailor) can design tartans for individuals in the customer's choice of colors. There is a worldwide mail order service.

Anyone who has an interest in the kilt-making process should make their way over to the store's five-story Tartan Weaving Mill, next to Edinburgh Castle, to see tartan cloth being woven.

MOLETA MUNRO

4 JEFFREY STREET

☎ (0131) 557 4800 · *www.moletamunro.com*

MON–SAT 10:30AM–6PM

THE SHOP'S TAGLINE IS SIMPLE YET AMBITIOUS: "EVERY-THING YOU'VE EVER WANTED FOR YOUR HOME." OWNERS Justin and Juliet Baddon place a special emphasis on local and regional designers and companies that are not widely known. They estimate that nearly seventy-five percent of the products at Moleta Munro are exclusive to the shop.

You'll find unique silkscreened lampshades and cushions by Johanna Basford, who hails from Aberdeenshire; lampshades, bags, and tea towels with a decidedly modernist bent by London-based Michelle Mason; lambswool cushions and tea cozies from the Scottish-based home and fashion accessories label Plora. The Baddons also stock vases, stoneware, half pint glasses, and candle holders, as well as salt and pepper shakers from a local designer, Camilla Prada, and many functional and stylish home products from Scandinavia.

WM CADENHEAD
WHISKY & RUM MERCHANT
ABERDEEN

ORIGINAL COLLECTION 462

ARDBEG	12yo	£33.30	14yo	£35.30
AUCHROISK	18yo	£36.30		
BEN NEVIS	16yo	£47.30		
BOWMORE	14yo	£33.80	15yo	£36.30
CAOL ILA	16yo	£37.30	17yo	£38.20
	12yo	£33.30	15yo	£36.40
CONVALMORE	26yo	£49.80		
CRAGGANMORE	16yo	£33.30	18yo	£34.20
CLYNELISH	17yo			
GLENFARCLAS	18yo			
GLENGLASSAUGH	23yo	£52.40		
GLENROTHES	13yo	£34.80	16yo	£36.10
GLEN SPEY	15yo	£43.8		
HIGHLAND PARK	18yo	£39.50	19yo	£40.20
LAPHROAIG	12yo	£33.40	15yo	£36.60
MACALLAN	17yo	£32.20		£45
MAGDUFF	16yo	£33.20		
TOBERMORY	13yo	£34.30		
MORTLACH	14yo	£35.50		
MORTLACH	14yo	£41.20		

CADENHEAD'S

172 CANONGATE

☎ (0131) 556 5864 · *www.wmcadenhead.com*

MON–SAT 10:30AM–5:30PM

CADENHEAD'S IS SMALL AND COZY. A WORN TARTAN RUG, WELL TROD BY THE FEET OF COUNTLESS VISITORS, covers creaky hardwood floors. A stained glass window from the company's early days (it was established in Aberdeen in 1842) is on full display as is the stern visage of Mr. Cadenhead himself, the original founder. Customers are encouraged to sample selections straight from one of five casks—and they do. Then, with drink in hand, they can sit at one of the three tables fashioned from casks.

As Scotland's oldest independent bottler and one of the oldest businesses along the Royal Mile, Cadenhead's takes its historical pedigree seriously. The firm's practice is to bottle whiskies from single casks in order to bring out their individual tastes. The whiskies are not subjected to any artificial or chemical processing, nor are coloring agents added, nor are they chill filtered, in contrast with the standard practice today. Other firms, according to manager Mark Davidson, try to obtain uniformity not only by chill filtering but also by mixing together the contents of numerous casks. He emphasizes that no two bottlings, even of whisky of the same age and from the same distillery, can (or should) taste and look identical.

In addition to more than 100 single malts, the shop stocks Cadenhead's Moidart, a vatted malt whisky; Cadenhead's Cognac; and

Cadenhead's Putachieside, a blended whisky. The Putachieside label depicts the view from the company's original premises in Aberdeen, an area known as Putachieside, which no longer exists. Cadenhead's also carries whiskies and rums from around the world.

The shop regularly sponsors a series of whisky tastings at a local pub, usually at the Tolbooth Tavern across the street (167 Canongate), which typically involves a selection of some of the more interesting and unusual bottlings.

THE OLD CHILDREN'S BOOKSHELF

175 CANONGATE · ☎ (0131) 558 3411

MON–FRI 10:30AM–5PM, SAT 10AM–5PM, SUN 11AM–4:30PM

THE NAME IS A BIT OF A MISNOMER AND MAY CAUSE THE PASSERBY TO DO A DOUBLE TAKE BUT ONCE inside this idiosyncratic bookshop, customers will find a surprisingly diverse and high-quality selection of children's books—of older vintage. Owner Shirley Neilson has assembled an impressive collection of children's classic literature. The shop has an especially strong selection of Scottish children's books, both fiction and nonfiction, including authors such as Kathleen Fidler, Naomi Mitchison, Nigel Tranter, Mollie Hunter, and Angus MacVicar. The renowned writers are here, too, including Lucy Maud Montgomery, Louisa May Alcott, Lewis Carroll, Rudyard Kipling, A. A. Milne, C. S. Lewis, and George MacDonald. Neilson also stocks science fiction and fantasy, the Hardy Boys, the early Oz books, World War II children's fiction, and prints from the best of children's illustrators.

In addition, she carries girls' school stories and boys' school stories, a particularly British genre of fiction set in boarding schools and often containing a moralistic bent. The best known example of the genre is probably Thomas Hughes's nineteenth-century *Tom Brown's Schooldays* but contemporary audiences may also recognize aspects of the tradition in the Harry Potter novels. She also carries World War II children's fiction and illustrated books and prints from the best of children's illustrators. A few of the more unusual items you'll find are biographies of children's book authors, childhood memoirs, and books about children's literature.

THE CARSON CLARK GALLERY

181–183 CANONGATE

☎ (0131) 556 4710

MON–SAT 10:30AM–5:30PM

WITH HIS NEAT BEARD AND HALF GLASSES PERCHED PRECARIOUSLY ON HIS NOSE, PAUL SCOTT CLARK LOOKS
every part the stereotypical image of
the somber collector, yet the gallery he
runs is hardly stuffy. The collection is
designed to appeal to all ages and to fit
all budgets. The shop, which Clark says
is Scotland's only specialist for original
antique maps and sea charts, showcases
a collection ranging from the sixteenth
to the nineteenth century; the earliest
item dates from 1493, the latest from
around 1900. "We've got it all, and
plenty of it," Clark says. Replicas will
cost, on average, £15–20, while original
work will fetch £1,000 or so.

Map collectors could spend many
hours here poring over what he has amassed; it's the kind of place that
encourages leisurely browsing. In addition to maps, Clark carries engrav-
ings, prints (especially of Old Edinburgh), and charts. Scotland is amply
represented, of course, but other countries and areas are here, too.

ESCOSSE,

QVI EST

LE XII. LIVRE

DE L'EUROPE.

THE SOAP CO.

263 CANONGATE

☎ (0131) 478 4244 · *www.thesoapcoedinburgh.co.uk*

DAILY 10AM–5:30PM

HANDMADE IN EDINBURGH USING NATURAL BOTANI-CALS, THE SOAP CO. BLENDS ITS OWN SOAP USING THE traditional cold press method, a method that retains the natural and moisturizing glycerin. After the soap is hand blended, it is wrapped or bottled "with care."

Some of the scents are named after prominent Scottish authors, such as Red Red Rose (for Robert Burns's poem) or Treasure Island (a combination of musk, lemon, and cinnamon, inspired by Robert Louis Stevenson's novel). Other soaps take their inspiration from traditional Scottish recipes. Cranachan is a fragrant aroma of raspberries, oats, cream, honey, and whisky, and a recipe actually comes with this particular bar of soap.

The Soap Co. also sells

bubble bath, body wash, shampoos, and conditioners. A mini-soap stack, consisting of five tiny square-shaped soaps, is a real charmer and undoubtedly will appeal to travelers, children, and children at heart.

RAGAMUFFIN

278 CANONGATE

☎ (0131) 557 6007 · *www.ragamuffinonline.co.uk*

MON–SAT 10AM–6PM, SUN NOON–5PM (APR–SEPT TIL 6PM)

RAGAMUFFIN WAS STARTED NEARLY THIRTY YEARS AGO ON THE ISLE OF SKYE. OWNER LESLEY ROBERTSON, an Edinburgh native, was still in school when she began designing and making clothing and jewelry and selling them to her friends. After graduation, she went to Skye on holiday and fell in love with the place—the physical beauty of it. Determined to stay, she opened her first shop in a falling down studio on the island before moving to another location at the Armadale pier, where it remains today. It wasn't until fifteen or so years later that she opened a second shop, this time along Edinburgh's Royal Mile, in the heart of the Old Town.

Ragamuffin sells designer knitwear, clothing, and accessories for men, women, and children, from throughout the United Kingdom, Ireland, and the Continent in a range of mostly natural fibers, including wool, silk, cotton, linen, and merino. Styles are eclectic, from simple t-shirts, trousers, and jackets to elegant dresses and coats.

Maybe it has something to do with Ragamuffin's origins, but Robertson seems to have a soft spot for artists from the Orkney Islands, including designer labels Tait & Style and Hume Sweet Hume. She also carries scarves by the Border-based designer Shirley Pinder; England's Sophie's Wild Woollens; and, from farther afield, Oska from Germany; knit-wear from Bolivia; and textiles from India.

In addition to carrying the work of more than fifty designers, Robertson also designs and makes her own collections of jackets and fleeces—stylish and functional clothing that is easy to wear and care for—under the Angels Don't Trudge label, much of it inspired by the landscape of Skye.

LENORE LIPPETT

11 ST. MARY'S STREET

☎ (0131) 557 0423 · NO CREDIT CARDS

MON–SAT 11AM–5PM

SUN DURING THE EDINBURGH FESTIVAL

AFTER THIRTY YEARS OF RUNNING THIS ECLECTIC ANTIQUES STORE JUST OFF THE ROYAL MILE, OCTOGE-narian Lenore Lippett has amassed a range of curios that could keep you browsing for ages. It's the ideal place to pick up a European antique at a reasonable price, for Lenore says she runs her shop more for pleasure than for profit. Lenore's specialties are European ceramics and early costume jewelry, but there are also pictures and textiles on hand. It's a tiny space—there isn't room for more than a handful of customers—which only adds to its charm. If the shop isn't busy, she will be able to relate a sweeping history of her beloved Edinburgh—she was once a tour guide.

FARMERS MARKET

CASTLE TERRACE

SAT 9AM–2PM

CASH ONLY

A NOT-TO-BE-MISSED PART OF EDINBURGH LIFE IS THE FARMERS MARKET, HELD EVERY SATURDAY IN THE shadow of Edinburgh Castle. Local producers from around the city set up their stalls early in the morning to provide visitors and residents with a wide choice of food and other necessities. Don't be put off by the long queues—they testify to the popularity of the market. You can buy local organically grown vegetables and eggs from East Coast Organics or fill up your suitcases with deliciously scented handmade soaps to take back as presents. Border Tablet is often here, too, giving out samples of this tradi-

tional and very sweet Scottish confectionery. Not for the health conscious, its main ingredients are butter and sugar—and lots of it—and condensed milk. In addition, you may also find a local chocolate maker, a local jam producer, and a stall selling woolen goods—you never know.

Even if you aren't looking for gifts or souvenirs, the market is still worth a visit. You can find lunch at stalls offering freshly roasted meat sandwiches or handmade crisps (better known as potato chips on the other side of the ocean). Or, if you are early, stop by the stall selling porridge, Scotland's traditional breakfast.

THE JOLLY JUDGE

7 James Court, Lawnmarket ☎ (0131) 225 2669
Pub lunches daily · Inexpensive

One of the most atmospheric pubs in Edinburgh, the Jolly Judge is a favorite of locals and tourists alike (as well as journalists and legal workers). With its exposed beams, low ceilings, and fireplace, the pub is warm and cozy—the perfect place for a light lunch or a pint or two.

DEACON BRODIES TAVERN

435 Lawnmarket ☎ (0131) 225 6531
Lunch and dinner daily · Inexpensive

Sure, this traditional-style pub is a bit of a tourist trap but it's an interesting tourist trap. After all, it is named after William Brodie: respectable citizen by day, criminal by night. Brodie inspired Robert Louis Stevenson's classic novella, *The Strange Case of Dr. Jekyll and Mr. Hyde*. Pub food is available downstairs while there is a more formal restaurant upstairs. Any way you look at it, it's a fun place.

CREELERS

3 Hunter Square ☎ (0131) 220 4447
Mon, Thur-Sun, Noon-2:30pm, 5:30-10:30pm; Tues, Wed 5:30-10:30pm
Lunch and dinner · Moderate

This excellent restaurant originated on the Isle of Arran, offering a beguiling mixture of simplicity and elegance. It specializes in fresh seafood but it usually has a few meat and vegetarian dishes on the menu, too. Owners Tim and Fran James have their roots in the West Coast; Tim near the Mull of Kintyre, Fran from the Oban area.

DAVID BANN

56-58 St Mary's Street ☎ (0131) 556 5888
Daily from 11am to 1am · Moderate

Off the Royal Mile, David Bann is a well-respected and innovative vegetarian restaurant that offers sophisticated fare at good value. Its modern décor matches the contemporary panache of its imaginative dishes (risotto of beetroot, kale, and blue cheese, or chili and smoked cheese tortilla tartlet with chocolate sauce). Brunch (around £6) is served every Saturday and Sunday until 5pm.

CLARINDA'S TEAROOM

69 Canongate ☎ (0131) 557 1888
Breakfast, lunch, afternoon tea · Inexpensive

A lovely place along the Royal Mile for a traditional afternoon tea, complete with lace tablecloth and fine china. The tearoom is named after one of many of Robert Burns's love interests, Agnes Craig MacLehose. Burns gave her the sobriquet of Clarinda.

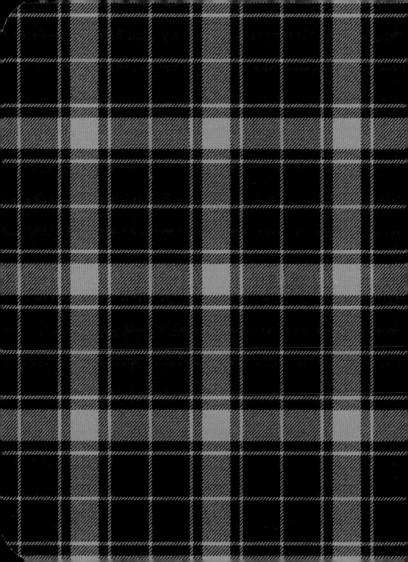

WALK 2 ✦ THE GRASSMARKET

JOYCE FORSYTH

42 CANDLEMAKER ROW

☎ (0131) 220 4112 · *www.joyceforsyth.co.uk*

TUES–SAT 10AM–5:30PM

JOYCE FORSYTH IS AN INDEPENDENT SCOTTISH DESIGNER OF KNITWEAR. WORKING OUT OF ONE ROOM IN AN ATMOSPHERIC 300-year-old building, she can often be seen at one of the two knitting machines that sit behind her desk. Trained in woolen textiles at Gray's School of Art in Aberdeen, Forsyth designs and produces easy-to-wear garments using natural yarns, including sweaters, tops, jumpers, scarves, and hats. Her designs boast bright and vibrant colors in various shades of red, blue, gold, green, and brown. She also accepts orders for custom items. Forsyth offers contemporary knitwear with plenty of flair and personality—a melding of the modern with the traditional—that should appeal to anyone who appreciates originality and freshness.

FABHATRIX

13 COWGATEHEAD

☎ (0131) 225 9222 · *www.fabhatrix.com*

MON–SAT 10:30AM–6PM

CLOSED SUN EXCEPT DURING FESTIVAL AND CHRISTMAS SEASON

AS YOU WALK INTO FABHATRIX THE IMPRESSION IS OF A VERITABLE SEA OF FLOATING HATS, AS IF BOBBING UP and down on the ocean. There are hats for both men and women, for special occasions or everyday wear. Most of the hats are handmade by owner Fawns Reid, at her downstairs workshop.

All together, Reid carries about 300 hats (most sell within the £29–45 range), as well as accessories, many created by younger generations of Scots or English designers, milliners, jewelers, and textile artists. Fabhatrix stocks classic styles as well as quirky, innovative work. The collection includes fedoras, bowlers, tricorn hats, caps, and top hats in Harris tweed, cotton, and velvet. Dyed-wool hats come with matching scarves and wraps; tweed hats are often finished off with feathers or hatpins. Also available are accessory items such as hair clasps, felt scarves, and brooches.

Some of these items are made exclusively for Fabhatrix. Textile artist Jenny Garner, for example, creates handbags that are made from recycled tweed and tartan with such embellishments as vintage buttons, silk, lace, and ribbons. Another artist, Jane McAllister, a sporran maker by trade, creates quirky jewelry, using figurines, thimbles, and collectible teaspoons.

ARMSTRONG'S

83 GRASSMARKET

☎ (0131) 220 5557 · *www.amstrongsvintage.co.uk*

MON–THUR 10AM–5:30PM, FRI & SAT 10AM–6PM, SUN NOON–6PM

SPREAD OUT OVER THREE BIG ROOMS, EDINBURGH'S LARGEST VINTAGE SHOP STOCKS WOMEN'S AND MEN'S clothing from every decade since the 1980s and some dating as far back as the Victorian era. The music of the Rolling Stones and Dolly Parton blasts over the sound system, putting you in a perfectly comfortable shopping or browsing mood.

Serendipity plays a big part in the shop's eclectic appeal. You never know what you may find here from one day to the next, but on one visit you may come across ball gowns, 1960s day dresses, 1970s checked double-breasted trench-style jackets, vintage Highlandwear and kilts, antique uniforms, and all types of shoes from stilettos to platforms. What's more, the opinionated comments on the sales tags are every bit as entertaining and idiosyncratic as the shop itself. Consider: "Right, so someones wearin flares. Suddenly they stumble over some tripwire (layed by pesky monkeys). Safe to say, they can't be here to tell the tale, but they left these to buy it for them… tripwire flares. Yeh!"

HAWICK CASHMERE

HAWICK CASHMERE IS ONE OF SCOTLAND'S LEADING CASHMERE SPECIALISTS AND ALSO ONE OF ITS OLDEST. Founded in 1874 in Hawick, its headquarters are still located in that Border town's original nineteenth-century Trinity Mill, where it employs 150 people and is said to be the largest cashmere factory in Scotland. The company's Grassmarket shop, one of only twelve of the company's retail stores in the UK, is spacious and airy, spread out over several rooms.

Hawick stocks jumpers, scarves, knitted wraps, and women's and men's cashmere sweaters. The vibrant colors include orange, red, bottle green, heather, purple, pink, green, grey, cream, and black. Although many of the styles are traditional, Hawick's also carries more contemporary styles. Recently, the company hired a Japanese designer, Masayo Urano, whose designs might include puffy or bell sleeves or a rolled collar.

BILL BABER

66 GRASSMARKET

☎ (0131) 225 3249 · *www.billbaber.com*

MON–SAT 9AM–5:30PM

CLOSED SUN EXCEPT DURING FESTIVAL

Bill Baber emphasizes that each piece on display is a wearable work of art. Made by hand, with color variations, no two items are alike. "We've never made the same garment twice," says Baber, who works in tandem with his wife Helen. She is the designer while he handles the technical aspects. Typically, their shop carries about 400 different garments. Although the clothing, which includes sweaters, jackets, and shells, tends to be casual and comfortable, it can easily be dressed up with accessories. Many of their pieces incorporate their patented design, a Celtic knot motif.

The shop has been open since 1977. The Baber studio is in the back of the store. Colorful yarn — Belfast linen, merino, Spanish silk, and cotton — sits on rows of shelves. Don't be afraid to pop your head in for a look.

CLARKSONS

87 WEST BOW

☎ (0131) 225 8141 · *www.clarksonsedinburgh.co.uk*

MON–SAT 10:30AM–5:30PM

CURVING, PRECIPITOUS, AND LEADING DOWN TO THE FAMOUS GRASSMARKET, BOW STREET IS ONE OF THE oldest and most atmospheric streets in Edinburgh. Give yourself plenty of time to gaze in the windows of the various retailers as you make your way down to Clarksons, a family-run jewelry shop housed in a picturesque building that dates back to circa 1720.

Clarksons opened in 1958, and is still run by Ian and Nora Clarkson and their sons, Michael and Keith. More than eighty percent of the items on display—they specialize in contemporary and Celtic-style jewelry—have been made on site by Michael, who graduated from the Glasgow School of Art, and his young team of craftspeople and jewelers, all of whom have been trained in-house (the workshop is upstairs). Most pieces are made using only precious metals and gemstones.

The Clarksons use traditional materials such as sterling silver, gold, and platinum. Many of their offerings are either one-of-a-kind pieces or produced in small runs. Commissions are regularly undertaken.

PINE & OLD LACE

46 VICTORIA STREET

☎ (0131) 225 3287

MON–TUES, THUR–SAT 10:30AM–5PM

JUST OFF THE GRASSMARKET, WEST BOW TURNS INTO VICTORIA STREET, A LOVELY COBBLESTONE LANE OF distinctive shop after distinctive shop. Buildings are painted in various colors: terracotta, pastel blue, pink.

Stepping inside tiny Pine & Old Lace is like stepping into a home at the turn of the last century, or perhaps even longer ago. The shop specializes in antique linen and lace as well as homemade furniture and kitchen fittings. Owner Sharon Fujimoto has been collecting for years—and it shows. Every square inch of the shop is devoted to lace and all of it is old, some more than a hundred years. You'll find handkerchiefs, dressing gowns, embroidered pillows, and bloomers, found at house sales, antique shows, or through a variety of private sources.

TOTTY ROCKS

40 VICTORIA STREET
☎ (0131) 226 3232 · *www.tottyrocks.co.uk*
MON–SAT 10AM–6PM, SUN 11AM–4PM

THIS SMALL GRASSMARKET SHOP REFLECTS THE WORLD VIEW, PHILOSOPHY, AND PANACHE OF ITS TWO YOUNG owners, Lynsey Miller and Holly Campbell. The store really does live up to its rock'n'roll–style name and the women's now considerable reputations. The duo's good taste is tempered with a bit of whimsy and an ample dose of cheeky good humor.

Both Miller and Campbell graduated with degrees in fashion design from Edinburgh College of Art and worked for design companies in London, Paris, Milan, and Hong Kong before opening Totty Rocks in 2006.

Totty Rocks is primarily a women's wear label although it does also carry a fair selection of men's and children's clothing. Quite often their patterns are full of quiet surprises; attention to detail is an important feature of their design philosophy. Their quirky sense of humor is evident, too, in a fur purse in the

[53]

shape of a traditional Scottish sporran (complete with fringe) or a black leather purse in the shape of a cat. Other designs veer between modern and traditional: you might find a simple black satin shirtdress or a mackintosh lined with a quirky print.

DEMIJOHN

32 VICTORIA STREET

☎ (0131) 225 3265 · *www.demijohn.co.uk*

MON–SAT 10AM–6PM, SUN 12:30PM–5PM

I N THIS "LIQUID DELI," AS OWNER ANGUS FERGUSON CALLS IT, CUSTOMERS CHOOSE AMONG SINGLE MALT WHISKIES, spirits, and liqueurs, as well as olive oils, vinegars, and spices, which are then packaged in narrow-necked, often beautifully colored bottles known as demijohns. What makes Demijohn so much fun is that customers are

allowed to taste the liquid treasures before buying them, then choose among a selection of demijohns. Scottish liqueurs typically available include a raspberry vodka from East Lothian, made from local berries, and Jago's vanilla vodka cream liqueur, a smooth and creamy drink made in Shetland that combines cream, Madagascar vanilla, and Blackwood's vodka. Moniack Castle Winery's mead hails from Invernessshire (Moniack is the only winery in Scotland). Ferguson also stocks products from other areas of Britain such as a black cherry liqueur from Wales and a Lyme Bay butterscotch cream liqueur made with Devonshire cream. Vinegars come in various flavors, including raspberry, apple, and red currant.

WALKER SLATER

20 VICTORIA STREET

☎ (0131) 220 2636 · *www.walkerslater.com*

MON–SAT 10AM–6PM, THUR 10AM–7 PM

WALKER SLATER'S LINE OF MEN'S CLOTHING WAS FIRST DESIGNED AND PRODUCED IN 1989 FROM A CONVERTED byre (or barn) in the Highlands. The Edinburgh store opened in 1993, specializing in both ready-to-wear and custom suits, jackets, trousers, and shirts. Although inspired by the terrain and colors of the Highlands, and using traditional cloths, the company creates contemporary styles. Walker Slater also carries knitwear in a variety of weights and styles; as well as Mackintosh rainwear (hand-made in Scotland from rubberized cotton), mill-washed linen clothing, garments made of cotton twill and canvas, as well as braces (suspenders), caps (their own design), Dents gloves, Cheaney shoes, and Holliday & Brown neckwear.

But tweeds remain the house specialty—all kinds of tweeds from Border to Shetland to Harris to Donegal—including tweed jackets that are lightweight and casual yet dressy enough for most occasions. The traditional components of the three-piece suits (jacket, vest, trousers) are sold separately to mix and match.

THE OLD TOWN BOOKSHOP

8 VICTORIA STREET

☎ (0131) 225 9237 · *www.oldtownbookshop.co.uk*

MON–SAT 10:30AM–5:45PM

A HANDWRITTEN SIGN LOCATED TO THE RIGHT OF THE DOOR ENCOURAGES PASSERSBY WITH A LITERARY BENT to step inside. "Old Books Maps & Prints," it promises—and it doesn't disappoint. A general secondhand bookstore, with some antiquarian titles, this musty and very narrow, one-room shop is especially strong in art, architecture, and photography. Other specialties include a nice collection of old Edinburgh maps and prints, books on Robert Burns, poetry, gardening, and a large Scottish section, especially Scots literature. Also here are titles on birding, history, travel, lighthouses, children's books, and various literary paraphernalia. It's a quirky and eccentric kind of place where one could spend a pleasant hour (or two) filing through the selection of prints and maps or perusing the shelves for out-of-print or just plain unusual titles.

GODIVA BOUTIQUE

9 WEST PORT

☎ (0131) 221 9212 · *www.godivaboutique.co.uk*

MON–SAT 10:15AM–6PM, SUN 1–5PM

MON–SAT 11AM–7:30PM, SUN NOON–5PM (SUMMER)

"FOR THE DISCERNING AND DETERMINEDLY DIFFERENT" IS THE GUIDING PRINCIPLE OF THIS SHOP, WHICH HAS been called Edinburgh's "most original independent boutique." Godiva stocks new items, vintage items, and new items made from vintage fabrics. Some of the clothing is made by owner Fleur Mackintosh who works in a downstairs warehouse/studio, where she keeps a collection of vintage fabrics and guarantees that "we don't make the same things twice." Customers can choose vintage fabrics, or new; almost everything is made to measure and at no extra cost.

The front room consists largely of clothes designed by art school graduates, many from the Edinburgh College of Art, which is located across the street; you'll also find items from local artists and up-and-coming designers from throughout the UK. Look for the work of Rowan Joy McIntosh, who mixes vintage and modern fabrics, and that of Becky Bolton and Louise Chappell, whose label is Good Wives and Warriors. Bolton and Chappell's bags, purses, shopping bags, and laptop bags all are unique and handmade.

Don't forget to check out the back room. Vintage items are plentiful there, including tops, dresses, and boots.

HERMAN BROWN

151 WEST PORT

☎ (0131) 228 2589

MON–SAT 12–6PM, SUN 1–5PM (SUMMER)

ANNA NICHOLSON'S SHOP IS FULL OF SURPRISES AND REFLECTS HER PERSONALITY AND ECLECTIC TASTES. She has found inspiration in the things that "…people chuck out. People are constantly bringing things to me," she says. "One woman recently brought in eight fur coats." She describes her shop as carrying everything from retro to modern clothing, as well as jewelry and accessories, from the 1920s to the present day. She finds most of the items at antique fairs, through dealers, or private sources. In addition to clothing, Nicholson carries 1940s and 1950s jewelry, sunglasses, cashmere, fur coats from the 1940s through the 1970s, and shoes.

BOOKSHOPS OF THE WEST PORT

FURTHER ALONG THE GRASSMARKET IS A STREET CALLED THE WEST PORT THAT CONTAINS A NUMBER OF SMALL secondhand and antiquarian bookshops. ANDREW PRINGLE, BOOK-SELLER (No. 62, 0131 228 8880)—it's the one with the attractive red door—is a well-organized and well-lit one-room shop that carries a strong general selection but also has a nice collection of old prints and maps with an emphasis on Scottish titles. Pringle is strong in literature, history, art, bibliography, heraldry, and military.

The one-room PETER BELL, BOOKSELLER (No. 68, 0131 229 0562) has a good, general stock of secondhand and antiquarian academic books, but owner Bell's strong suits are Victorian books and pamphlets, especially imprints; pamphlets in general (including sermons); and academic texts in history, literature, and philosophy. He also likes Scottish history and literature and publications by Edinburgh University Press circa 1953–1987, as well as Penguin Classics.

Two rooms make up ARMCHAIR BOOKS (No. 72–74, 0131 229 5927). The shop has a large Victorian and Scottish collection as well as titles on arts and crafts, architecture, theater, classics, and literary criticism but also an extensive general stock of secondhand and some antiquarian books. General literature and science fiction are on the shelves, too.

EDINBURGH PORT BOOKS (No. 145–47 0131 229 4431) consists of three small rooms including the Scottish room which is filled with a large number and wide range of Scottish titles. It's an old-fashioned, musty kind of place with a few chairs and worn carpets—the kind of bookshop where you can spend hours just browsing through the shelves. A lackadaisical border collie sits by the owner's desk, seemingly oblivious to the crush of people who walk in and out, clutching their handfuls of books. The shop carries titles on World War I, World War II, literature and poetry, music, travel, and Victoriana as well as sections on Scots language/Gaelic, architecture, history, and literature/fiction. You'll also find a large collection of titles on both Glasgow and Edinburgh.

WALK 2 ✦ FOOD & DRINK

THE ELEPHANT HOUSE

21 George IV Bridge ☎ (0131) 220 5355
Open 8-11pm daily for breakfast, lunch, and dinner

Supposedly it's the "birthplace" of Harry Potter—J. K. Rowling is said to have written one of her early Potter novels in the back room of this coffeehouse. Potter or no Potter, the Elephant House, just off Victoria Street, is a busy hangout and a good choice for coffee, tea, cakes, and sandwiches. Wine by the glass or bottle is also available. The Elephant House is reportedly a favorite haunt of Edinburgh authors, including Ian Rankin and Alexander McCall Smith.

THE WHITE HART INN

34 Grassmarket ☎ (0131) 226 2806
Lunch and dinner · Inexpensive

Said to be Edinburgh's oldest surviving pub (circa 1516), this friendly Grassmarket watering hole has quite a literary pedigree. Robert Burns stayed here in 1791. In September 1803, William and Dorothy Wordsworth stopped by for one night ("It was not noisy, and tolerably cheap"). More notoriously, in 1828, William Burke and William Hare enticed a number of their fellow patrons—seventeen victims to be exact—back to their nearby lodgings where they murdered them and sold their corpses to Dr. Knox at Edinburgh's Medical School for dissection. The story inspired Robert Louis Stevenson to write his short story "The Body Snatcher."

The White Hart Inn has a varied menu, serving soups, salads, sandwiches, bangers and mash (such as pork and leek sausages), and vegetarian haggis (mixed vegetables with oatmeal and spices and mashed turnips and potatoes). Great atmosphere, too, with its wooden tables and chairs, cozy, beamed ceiling, and fireplace. Live folk music on Tuesday nights.

GREYFRIARS BOBBY BAR

34 Candlemaker Row ☎ (0131) 225 8328

Lunch & dinner · Inexpensive

Popular with tourists and students (the University of Edinburgh is a short walk away), Greyfriars is a friendly and casual tavern serving pub food. What makes it special is its place in local Edinburgh lore. Edinburgh police officer John Gray, who died of tuberculosis in 1858, is buried in Greyfriars Kirkyard, a mere stone's throw away. His faithful dog, a Skye terrier named Bobby, is said to have watched over his grave for the next fourteen years, until the dog's own death in 1872. A statue of the loyal canine stands on the street outside the pub.

SCOTTISH CHEESES

EVERYONE KNOWS ABOUT FRENCH CHEESE, ENGLISH CHEESE, AND EVEN IRISH CHEESE, BUT SCOTTISH CHEESE HAS A much lower profile, despite the fact that Scotland produces some of the world's finest. In recent years, there has been a revival in artisanal and specialty cheeses made using traditional methods. Here is a brief list of some cheeses to look for while shopping or dining:

Bishop Kennedy: Strong and sticky with a runny yellow center; washed in malt whisky to produce a characteristic orange-red crust.

Caboc: Cream-cheese-like in texture, a Highland cheese typically rolled in toasted pinhead oatmeal and shaped like a log.

Cairnsmore: A dry, hard cheese from Galloway with a nutty taste.

Criffel: From Dumfries; smooth and tangy with a floral, herb-like taste.

Crowdie: A Highland cheese, similar in texture to cottage cheese, made from skimmed cow's milk.

Dunlop: A traditional cloth-bound cheese matured for approximately nine months; nutty flavor accompanied by a moist texture.

Dunsyre Blue: A handmade cheese, sister to Lanark Blue (see below), made from unpasteurized Ayrshire cow's milk and known for its sharp flavor.

Iona Cromak: A firm but creamy curd cheese with a crumbly center whose rind is soaked in whisky from the Isle of Mull's Tobermory Distillery.

Isle of Mull: A cheddar-style cheese that is paler in color, softer in

texture, and sharper in flavor than traditional cheddar.

Lanark Blue: Often referred to as the Scottish equivalent of Roquefort. Soft and flavorful, it is handmade in a farmhouse creamery from unpasteurized ewes' milk.

Loch Arthur: A Scottish cheddar, milder than English cheddar.

Orkney Farmhouse Cheese: Buttery and mellow.

Strathdon Blue: A Highland cheese with a spicy flavor.

Sweet Milk: Smooth and nutty with a hint of lemon; made from organic Ayrshire milk.

A good place to sample and buy Scottish cheeses is at Iain Mellis, Cheesemonger. The full and underappreciated glory of Scottish cheese is on display here. As soon as you walk into this tiny, narrow shop, you smell their full pungency. As a traditional cheesemaker of the old school, Iain sells only those considered farmhouse cheeses, usually made with milk from the cheesemaker's own herd.

Also on sale are cheeses from beyond Scotland, cheese wedding cakes, baguettes, Adamson oatcakes from Fife, blossom honey fron Perthshire, and marmalades. Iain, who has been working in the cheese industry in various capacities since 1979, owns several stores in Edinburgh (30a Victoria Street; 0131 226 6215; 205 Bruntsfield Place, 0131 447 8889; 6 Bakers Place, 0131 225 6566) and one in Glasgow (492 Great Western Road, 0141 339 8998).

Iain J. Mellis

CHEESEMONGER
SCOTLAND'S FINEST
FARMHOUSE
CHEESES

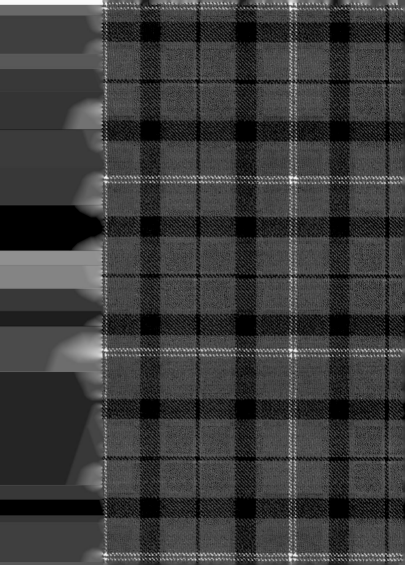

WALK 3 ✦ NEW TOWN

JOSEPH BONNAR

72 THISTLE STREET

☎ (0131) 226 2811 · *www.josephbonnar.co.uk*

MON–SAT 10:30AM–5PM

WITH ITS RICH DARK GREEN WALLS AND JEWEL BOX-LIKE INTERIOR, JOSEPH BONNAR, EDINBURGH'S premier antique and period jewelry store, is full of unusual and unexpected treasures. The shop specializes in diamonds and fine stones and has

the largest selection of antique jewelry in Scotland, including brooches, necklaces, and pendants. You may find late Victorian or 1920s diamond brooches, a late nineteenth-century gold- and enamel-set portrait brooch of Queen Victoria, a nineteenth-century silver Russian snuff box, antique flasks or, perhaps, a silver mounted stone-set dirk with MacPherson crest, circa 1870. Prices range from less than £100 to £95,000.

JANE DAVIDSON

52 THISTLE STREET

☎ (0131) 225 3280 · *www.janedavidson.co.uk*

MON–SAT 9:30AM–6PM, THUR 9:30AM–7PM

GENERATIONS OF MOTHERS AND DAUGHTERS HAVE BEEN COMING HERE EVER SINCE THE SHOP WAS ESTABLISHED in 1969; indeed, generations of visitors from around the world have also made their way here. *Harpers & Queen* magazine recently voted the store as one of the top twenty-five boutiques in the world. Housed on

three floors of a Georgian townhouse along a cobblestone New Town street, Jane Davidson may carry the big names in contemporary women's fashion, including Nanette Lepore, Paul & Joe, and Diane von Furstenberg, but she also supports Scottish-based designers such as Cameron Taylor, who makes luxury cashmere knitwear, including cardigans, jackets, coats, tunic dresses, and tunic tops.

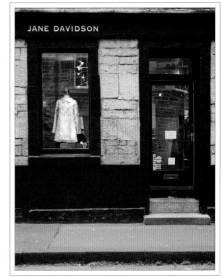

GAMEFISH

6A HOWE STREET

☎ (0131) 220 6465 · *www.gamefishltd.co.uk*

MON–FRI 9:30AM–6PM, SAT 10AM–5PM

A S ITS NAME INDICATES, GAMEFISH SPECIALIZES IN FLY FISHING TACKLE, REELS, FLY LINES, WADERS, WADING staffs, boots, and country clothing. The shop's fly rods and salmon rods are highly rated by ghillies—fishing and hunting guides—all over Scotland. Owner Nick Armstead and his staff would also be pleased to recommend and arrange organized fly fishing expeditions both within the United Kingdom and beyond. In addition, they can offer casting instructions and are especially patient when offering advice—selecting your first fishing rod or reel—to beginners.

PETER JOHNSTON

40 QUEEN STREET

☎ (0131) 225 4318 · *www.peter-johnston.co.uk*

MON–SAT 9:30AM–6PM

EVERYTHING ABOUT PETER JOHNSTON'S CUSTOMIZED TAILORING AND SHIRT-MAKING STORE IN THE NEW Town speaks of a quiet elegance. Everything on offer—which includes shirts, ties, cuff links, shoes, scarves, and gloves—reflects the understated, timeless dignity that is the hallmark of the collection. As for Peter Johnston himself, he is a top-notch designer who makes no effort to disguise the fact that he is a Glasgow boy, hailing from the village of Houston on the outskirts of the city. In 2005, he launched his own label and, in 2006, he opened the first stand-alone Peter Johnston store in Edinburgh.

With the exception of the Italian luggage, everything at the store is made in the United Kingdom. Each piece of clothing is hand cut and hand sewn. The choice of garments includes shirts, suits, jackets, trousers, vests, as well as eveningwear and morning and top coats. Tailored shirts come in eight collar styles and eight cuff styles and maintain traditional features such as removable collar stays. The clothing may be inspired by classic designs but Johnston also tries to appeal to a modern sensibility. Thus, even his "pared-down look" manages to be casual yet sophisticated.

STEWART CHRISTIE & CO.

63 QUEEN STREET

☎ (0131) 225 6639

MON–SAT 9AM–5:30PM

STEWART CHRISTIE & CO. IS A GENTLEMEN'S OUTFITTER OF THE OLD-FASHIONED KIND. IT IS THE THIRD OLDEST shop in Edinburgh and has been a family-run business since it opened more than 230 years ago. The shop is staffed by young men who are polite and restrained in a typical Scottish way; expect the door to be opened for you and to be called "madam" or "sir."

The shop offers custom tailoring, Highland dress, riding wear, and saddlery. There are old-fashioned but immaculate glass cabinets displaying shirts and ties, and the walls are hung with everything you need for a day on a country estate. Toward the back of the shop are rows upon rows of suits; there are also hats and handkerchiefs.

EDE & RAVENSCROFT

46 FREDERICK STREET

☎ (0131) 225 6354 · *www.edeandravenscroft.co.uk*

MON–FRI 9AM–5:30PM, SAT 9:30AM–5:30PM

EDE AND RAVENSCROFT IS A CELEBRATED BRITISH FIRM, ONE OF THE OLDEST IN THE UNITED KINGDOM, RENOWNED for its shirt making and robe making traditions. The Edinburgh branch has been serving a loyal clientele for generations.

Ede and Ravenscroft have been robe makers and tailors since 1689 when the Shudall family was commissioned to create the robes for the coronation of William and Mary; the firm has produced ceremonial robes for every coronation since. The firm serves as robe makers to the current Queen Elizabeth and makes judicial and academic robes as well, yet the backbone of the firm's business is the craft of wig making, for barristers and judges. Ede and Ravenscroft offers a personal tailoring service for suits and shirts. In addition to its custom shirts, the company also sells handmade ties.

THE THRIE ESTAITS

THE ECLECTIC AND QUIRKY ANTIQUE AND COLLECTIBLE OBJECTS IN THIS CHARMINGLY CHAOTIC SHOP REFLECT the personality of owner Peter Powell, a gregarious fellow who has been collecting since attending art school, as he says, "many years ago." There's no telling what you will find in his two small, cluttered rooms. Powell doesn't like to be pinned down but the Thrie Estaits specializes mostly in decorative and historic objects (such as period drinking glasses) as well as Dutch and Chinese pottery, contemporary and period paintings, brass items, hand-painted tiles, terracotta plaques, and bronze Buddha statues.

BELINDA ROBERTSON

13A DUNDAS STREET

☎ (0131) 557 8118 · *www.belindarobertson.com*

MON-FRI 9:30AM-6PM, SAT 10AM-6PM,

SUN NOON-5PM (SEASONAL)

BEFORE STARTING HER OWN CASHMERE LABEL, BELINDA ROBERTSON WORKED FOR SUCH FAMOUS LABELS AS NINA Ricci, Michael Kors, and Dior. Although her first retail outlet opened in London in 1998, the heart and soul of the company remains in Scotland. It is in Scotland where the collections are designed (by Robertson and Claire Ferguson) while they are produced in the Border town of Hawick. Her cashmere is known not only for its longevity, but because it doesn't pill easily, nor will it twist or loose its shape, says general manager Jane Grove-White.

In 2005, Belinda launched the White Label Collection of affordable designer knitwear that includes capes, cardigans, and coats. Her Cashmere Couture Collection is the more luxurious line. Belinda Robertson also carries menswear as well as a large selection of accessories—all in cashmere—including berets, wraps, stoles, cable hats, cable scarves, socks, shawls, gloves, and even underwear, as well as non-cashmere items, such as tops, slacks, and t-shirts.

WALK 3 ✦ FOOD & DRINK

HENDERSON'S

94 Hanover Street ☎ (0131) 225 2131

Restaurant, wine bar, bistro bar, bakery · Mon-Sat; bistro open Sun · Moderate

This longstanding, cafeteria-style vegetarian restaurant serves delicious meals (try the rich and filling nut loaf stuffed with hazelnuts and sweet potato mash in a rich savory stew). The more adventurous may want to sample the haggis crêpes, served in a creamy mustard sauce. There is live music every evening on the lower level. Wine bar too. A tried and true reliable.

THE MUSSEL INN

61-65 Rose Street ☎ (0131) 225 5979

Lunch & dinner daily · Expensive

Bright and airy with wood floors and butcherblock tables, the Mussel Inn specializes in fresh seafood with, as indicated by its name, mussels the house specialty. The mussels are served in a choice of broths, from traditional (white wine, garlic, and shallots) to leeks and even cider and cream.

THE CAFÉ ROYAL BAR / THE CAFÉ ROYAL CIRCLE BAR

17 West Register Street ☎ (0131) 556 1884 & ☎ (0131) 556 4124

Lunch & dinner · Moderate to expensive

An Edinburgh institution, this gorgeous Victorian bar and restaurant is worth a stop even if you pause just to admire its tiled floors, dark wood, brass fittings, a large circular bar, and Doulton tiles by the artist John Ayres.

There are two rooms; the bar, in addition to hand-pulled cask ales and malt whiskies, offers a limited menu while the adjacent oyster bar/restaurant specializes in fresh fish, shellfish, and game. A must.

KAY'S BAR

39 Jamaica Street ☎ (0131) 225 1858
Lunch · Inexpensive

Some may find this small and cozy pub a bit stuffy but for those who like their pubs on the old-fashioned side, Kay's is a low-key charmer. Housed in a former wine merchant's shop, it offers good and hearty food. Have a seat on one of its red cushions in the front or back room and while away the hours.

GLASS AND THOMPSON

2 Dundas Street ☎ (0131) 557 0909
Breakfast and lunch · Inexpensive

This casual deli/café with a modern décor serves absolutely terrific food. The mushroom and goat cheese tart is delicious, as is the moist stem ginger coconut ricotta cake. Wine too.

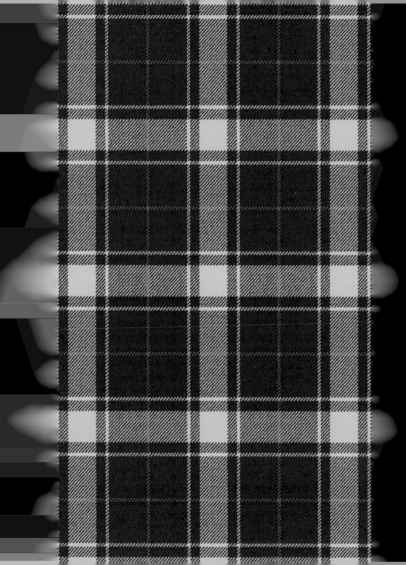

WALK 4 ✦ STOCKBRIDGE

DIANA FORRESTER

22 NORTH WEST CIRCUS PLACE

☎ (0131) 225 5877 · *www.dianaforrester.co.uk*

MON–SAT 10AM–6PM, SUN NOON–4PM

DIANA FORRESTER SPECIALIZES IN GIFTS AND ACCESSORIES FOR THE HOME AND GARDEN. WALK UP THE SIX stone steps, leaning ever so gently on the wrought-iron banisters, through a set of elegant grey doors and you will enter a shop that screams out—politely, of course—good taste. The shop, which consists of two levels, is located in a handsome Georgian building typical of the housing stock in this part of town. Like the architecture it evokes, Diana Forrester offers a subtle balance of class and commerce. Typical finds here include such quintessential British items as an iron wellie stand, umbrella stands, and actual wellies (in paisley and gingham) as well as glassware, cutlery, rattan baskets, bird cages, mouse and squirrel door wedges, and various styles of birdhouses.

NAPIER'S CLINIC

35 HAMILTON PLACE

☎ (0131) 315 2130 · *www.napiers.net*

MON 10AM-6PM, TUES-FRI 9AM-6PM,
SAT 9AM-5:30PM, SUN 12:30-4:30PM

ALTHOUGH ITS SERVICES APPEAR EXCEEDINGLY MODERN WITH AN EMPHASIS ON HERB AND PLANT REMEDIES, Napier's Clinic goes back to 1860, when its namesake, Duncan Napier, a Victorian botanist who held an intense fascination with plants and nature, opened his own shop. Originally a baker by trade, Napier became interested in herbal medicine after picking up a book on the subject at an Edinburgh market stall. Soon, he began to make medicines from herbs and plants collected from the surrounding area. Eventually—he had made a name for himself by this time—the Botanical Society of Edinburgh persuaded him to open his own shop.

After Napier's death at the age of 91, the business remained in the family for generations until medical herbalist Dee Atkinson took over in 1990. She returned to Napier's roots, researching the traditional recipes, slowly rebuilding and expanding their range. Today, Napier's consists of four branches (two in Edinburgh and two in Glasgow), offering a one-stop alternative to treat both body and mind. Napier's carries herbal products for various ailments, herbal teas, various supplements, herbal hair care, bath salts, body scrubs, hand and body cream, soaps, and therapy creams for skin conditions. Some of the recipes, such as scullcap, oat, and passionflower ("an old Napier's favorite for stress") date back to Duncan Napier's time.

CHIC & UNIQUE

8 DEANHAUGH STREET

☎ (0131) 332 9889 · *www.vintagecastjewellry.co.uk*

TUES–SAT 10:30AM–2PM, 2:30–5PM

CHIC & UNIQUE SPECIALIZES IN VINTAGE COSTUME JEWELRY AND ACCESSORIES. OWNER MOIRA TEALE carries bracelets (crystal, glass, bakelite, pearl), brooches (the Scottish

thistle, comedy and tragedy masks), necklaces, chokers, earrings, 1930s-style handbags, hatpins (Celtic, art nouveau), and vintage perfume bottles. The shop stocks cufflinks and other men's items such as a bakelite cigar holder.

Because they are so rare, Teale rents rather than sells tiaras. The tiaras range from 1820s Spain to 1930s Russia to French and Edwardian crystal tiaras to tiaras made as recently as the 1970s. If you have a particular piece in mind, Moira is happy to source it.

WALK 4 ✦ FOOD & DRINK

HERBIE OF EDINBURGH

1 Northwest Circus Place ☎ (0131) 226 7212

also at 66 Raeburn Place ☎ (0131) 332 9888 *(see below)*

HERBIE WEST END

7 William Street ☎ (0131) 226 6366

Breakfast and lunch · Moderate

Herbie's owners are avid advocates of the Slow Food movement. The Northwest Circus branch serves paninis, sandwiches, hummus, smoked salmon patés, and tuna melts as well as sweets, croissants, and smoothies. There is a juice bar; wine is served, too.

At 66 Raeburn Place, the Herbie of Edinburgh Bread Shop (0131 332 9888) makes its own bread. The types of bread vary from granary (the most popular) to organic wholemeal (malty and dense) to French country (flour, yeast, and water) to sweet and sour rye (80% wheat and 20% rye with caraway seeds and raised with baker's yeast) as well as 100% sourdough rye, Bavarian dark rye, and organic rye.

PATISSERIE FLORENTIN

5 Northwest Circle ☎ (0131) 220 0225
Breakfast & lunch · Inexpensive

This lovely café with a tasteful French atmosphere—red and white checked tablecloths, small round tables, posters—spread out over two rooms serves delicious quiches, salads, baguettes, toasties, baked potatoes, soups, and decadent sweets. Outdoor seating when weather permits.

THE BAILIE

2-4 St. Stephen Street ☎ (0131) 225 4673
Lunch & dinner · Moderate

This upscale basement pub located in the center of Stockbridge offers delicious and unusual food—not your typical pub fare—such as spicy chicken and chorizo penne in tomato and red wine sauce or tomato and fresh basil soup served with crusty bread and butter.

CHOCOLATE SHOPS

THE FUDGE HOUSE OF EDINBURGH

197 Canongate ☎ (0131) 556 4172 · *www.fudgehouse.co.uk*

Mon-Sat 10am-6pm, Sun 11am-6pm

The Disotto family has been making fudge for Edinburghers since 1949. The shop makes thirty flavors of fudge—all based on family recipes and all handmade—including hazelnut, almond cream, ginger, Italian nougat, mocha coffee and cream, rum and raisin, chocolate coconut, and, of course, whisky. In addition, you'll find butter tablet (a sort of Scottish toffee), coffee, scones, and seasonal light snacks. The Fudge House is also known for their homemade breads, unusual fillings of Parma ham, sun dried tomatoes, and roasted peppers, which can be eaten at one of the shop's three small tables.

PLAISIR DU CHOCOLAT

48 Thistle Street ☎ (0131) 225 9900

www.plaisirduchocolat.com

Tues-Sat 10am-6pm

After many years along the Royal Mile, Plaisir du Chocolat moved to the New Town in December 2007. The chocolatiers' approach when creating a new chocolate begins with a particular flavor and a theme, which may be a particular place (Africa, Asia, Arabia), cultural movements (art nouveau), literature (French novels of the nineteenth century), or history and mythology. Scotland itself has served as an inspiration on numerous occasions: "Laphroaig" is a dark ganache mixed with the flavor of Scotland's smokiest single malt; "Scotland," the bonbon created to celebrate the

reopening of the Scottish Parliament in 2004, consists of a white chocolate ganache with pure vanilla extract, Scottish heath and wildflower honey, and single malt whisky. All of the chocolates are handmade and gluten free. No sugar or preservatives are added. Plaisir du Chocolat also sells chocolate bars, hot chocolate, chocolate cakes, candied fruits in chocolate, and teas.

COCO OF BRUNTSFIELD

174 Bruntsfield Place ☎ (0131) 228 4526

www.cocochocolate.co.uk

Mon-Sat 10am-6pm

This tiny, narrow shop under a brown awning along busy Bruntsfield Place specializes in fine organic chocolate. All chocolates are designed in house by master chocolatiers based in Edinburgh using single origin chocolate from the Dominican Republic, Venezuela, and Madagascar; everything is made in the shop's kitchen.

Assorted creams are available in a variety of flavors (peppermint, rose, violet, orange, strawberry); the pink marc de champagne truffles are made from fresh cream chocolate and champagne ganache and then hand rolled in white and pink chocolate and edible rose petals. The handmade Organic Infusion Chocolate Bars come in a variety of exotic flavors (including chili pepper, cardamom and cinnamon, and organic milk chocolate with rose and ginger) and are presented in attractive boxes decorated with designs by local artists.

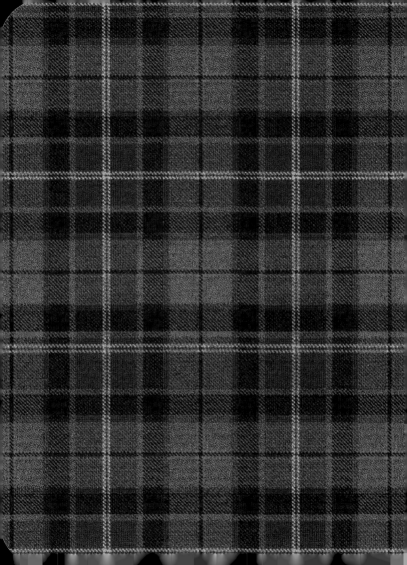

WALK 5 ✦ WILLIAM STREET

ARKANGEL

4 WILLIAM STREET

☎ (0131) 226 4466 · *www.arkangelfashion.co.uk*

MON-WED, FRI & SAT 10–5:30PM, THUR 10–6:30PM

ARKANGEL'S FASHION SENSIBILITY FAVORS QUIRKY TWISTS ON CLASSICAL THEMES. ON THEIR BIANNUAL buying trips, co-owners Lulu Benson and Janey Dalrymple look for clothes that are idiosyncratic and timeless, unusual but also practical. They carry exclusive designer clothing by artists from the UK and beyond as well as jewelry and accessories, including soaps, bath oils, and bath salts. Vintage and contemporary fashions share the same space. The look of the shop—hot pink door and window trim on the outside, purplish-pink floor inside—is indicative of the kind of lively atmosphere and funky milieu that Benson and Dalrymple have created.

HELEN BATEMAN

16 WILLIAM STREET

☎ (0131) 220 4495 · *www.helenbateman.com*

MON–SAT 9:30AM–6PM

ACCORDING TO ASSISTANT CLAIRE MCINTYRE, HELEN BATEMAN'S AMBITION IS "TO MAKE SHOES THAT ARE affordable, beautiful, and wearable. We're not high fashion as such," she says.

Bateman sources all the materials and designs the shoes herself. Her collection includes everyday shoes, special occasion shoes, pumps, mules, boots, sling-backs, slip-ons, and what she calls the Basics: comfortable shoes that can be worn year round, whether with skirts or slacks. Her shoes are known for their attention to detail: a flowery half boot with zipper may sport a purple velvet heel; an elegant day shoe might be made from grey tweed with burgundy suede and leather lining.

The shop also carries accessories, including scarves, belts, hats, shawls, jewelry. You'll also find purses, which might include handmade sterling silver evening purses, silver snake clutches in mock leather, or grey pinstripe wool handbags.

HOMER

18 WILLIAM STREET

☎ (0131) 226 4604 · *www.athomer.co.uk*

MON–SAT 9:30AM–5:30PM

HOMER, AN INTERIORS AND GARDEN SHOP, WAS FIRST HOUSED IN AN OLD BARN IN THE LOVELY PERTHSHIRE village of Aberfeldy. Owner Penny Kennedy has since opened this second shop, filled with practical and decorative accessories as well as furniture for the kitchen, the household, and the bedroom: tabletop items, lighting fixtures, old country furniture, china, linens, bedspreads, and throws, alongside smaller items such as lotions and soaps. Kennedy sources from all over Britain and Ireland as well as other European countries and around the world.

WALK 5 ✦ FOOD & DRINK

SCOTCH MIST

11a-13a William Street ☎ (0131) 226 3161
Lunch Noon-2:30PM, pre-theater 5-7PM, dinner 7-10PM · Expensive

Scottish cuisine with a continental twist. Although the restaurant offers fine dining, canny customers can enjoy superb value for their money with several options, including lunch (£6.95 for two courses or £5 for a main course); pre-theatre (two courses for £9.95); or a set dinner (single course for £12.95, two courses for £16.50, three courses for £19.50). The meals are inventive such as poached breast of chicken stuffed with Stornoway black pudding or vegetarian haggis with roasted root vegetables and apple sauce.

A ROOM IN THE WEST END

26 William Street ☎ 0131 226 1036
Open daily Noon-3pm for lunch & 5:30pm til late for dinner · Moderate

The owners emphasize fresh and affordable produce at this relaxed and friendly downstairs Scottish bistro. A typical entrée might be rosemary, apricot, and lamb mince topped with sour cream and chives; desserts might include brown-sugar-glazed chocolate tart with pistachio ice cream or iced passion fruit and raspberry terrine with blueberry compote. (Two courses cost £11.95, three courses, £13.95.) Although A Room in the West End has an optional BYOW policy (for wine and champagne only), a wider selection of drinks is available at the well-stocked upstairs bar, Teuchters.

WALK 6 ✦ BROUGHTON STREET

JOEY-D

54 BROADGHTON STREET
☎ (0131) 557 6672 · *www.joey-d.co.uk*
MON–SUN 10:30AM–6PM

JOEY-D SPECIALIZES IN RETRO CLASSIC HANDBAGS MADE FROM SECONDHAND ITEMS AS VARIOUS AS HARRIS TWEED jackets, bubblegum wrappers, and shoes—to name just a few possibilities. All of the work is handcrafted in Edinburgh by Joey Deacon, an affable

chap originally from Leicester. The reconstructed clothing he designs includes jackets, handbags, and shirts. Whether clothes or accessories, the items all have a robust and slightly subversive industrial look, a sort of in-your-face attitude, that is part punk, part military. The handbag made from a recycled Harris Tweed jacket will retain the pockets of the original and is embellished with fake bullets on the strap. Deacon realizes that it takes a certain type of person to wear his creations. As his logo indicates, they are designed for "men, women and urban wildlife."

CONCRETE WARDROBE

50A BROUGHTON STREET
☎ (0131) 558 7130
MON–SAT 10AM–6PM, SUN NOON–4PM

Owners James Donald and Fiona McIntosh have been showcasing work by Scottish-based or Scottish-trained designers for the past eight years; ninety percent of their stock is sourced in Scotland. Donald, a weaver, and McIntosh, a silkscreen printer, have managed to attract some of the top designers in the country.

The shop sits at the bottom of Broughton Street, a colorful avenue

of unusual shops and cafés. Once there, you can browse through a fascinating collection of artisan-based work, including jewelry, textiles, clothes, ceramics, glass, basketwork, and lights.

But be warned, it comes at a price. There are no mass-produced products here. Each item is handmade—think investment piece rather than impulse buy. But there are other offerings, such as ceramics or prints, at more moderate prices.

BLUE MOON CAFÉ

36 Broughton Street ☎ (0131) 556 2788

Breakfast, lunch, & dinner daily

The Blue Moon has simple, filling, and tasty food, from burgers to vegetarian fare. Good place for breakfast, a light lunch, dinner, or a late-night libation. Beer, wine, and spirits.

THE OLIVE BRANCH

91 Broughton Street ☎ (0131) 557 8589

Weekend brunch

A busy place for breakfast, lunch, and dinner—eggs, tartlets, salads, pastas, and light meals—as well as a popular weekend brunch. Tea is accompanied by a small almond cookie, a nice touch. The delicious crab, tomato, and tarragon tartlet is typical fare.

Glasgow

WALK 7 ✦ CITY CENTER

ARGYLL ARCADE

THE L-SHAPED ARGYLL ARCADE, WHICH LINKS BUSY ARGYLE AND BUCHANAN STREETS, COMES AS A BIT OF A SURPRISE to the unsuspecting visitor. Designed by John Baird in 1827 in the Parisian style (the arcade itself was built in 1904), the Argyll Arcade (the arcade and street names are often, but not always, spelled differently) is an example of early Victorian architecture in Glasgow. Called ferro-vitreous construction, the arcade juxtaposes exposed iron and glass lighting under what looks like (but is not) a skylight. The glass roof is supported with ornate "hammer-beam" roof trusses. Above the shops are framed windowed walls under a pitched roof. The Argyll Arcade is also one of Europe's oldest indoor shopping arcades as well as Scotland's first indoor shopping mall.

This indoor hallway is home to jeweler shop after jeweler shop—about thirty of them. Some started in Glasgow, others are national chains; two of the most interesting are described below.

JEWELRY SHOPS OF ARGYLL ARCADE

O F THE THIRTY OR SO JEWELRY SHOPS IN THE ARGYLL ARCADE, ONE OF THE OLDEST IS JAMES PORTER & SON (12–14 and 24–26 Argyll Arcade; 0141 221 5855; www.james-porter. co.uk), a member of the company of master jewelers, specializing in diamond rings, jewelry, and watches. The original shop is at Number 24–26. The premises have been expanded over the years; a clock showroom is upstairs. The second shop at the 12–14, has an extensive collection of estate diamond rings and jewelry.

What sets James Porter & Son apart from the rest of the Argyll Arcade jewelers though is its fine selection of quaiches. Historically, quaiches are Highland drinking vessels for whisky or brandy. They are distinguished by their two handles, known as lugs (Scots for ears), and made in a variety of sizes, from the smallest for drinking to the largest for ceremonial use. James Porter & Son has them available in sterling silver, silver-plate, and pewter, at a variety of prices. The company also stocks unusual flasks such as a Charles Rennie Mackintosh-style flask, a Celtic-style flask, and a St. Andrew's Old Course flask.

Michael James (4 Argyll Arcade, 0141 248 5666) offers jewelry as well as valuation and repair services. The shop's collections include Charles Rennie Mackintosh-inspired brooches, necklaces, and bracelets. Among the more striking items is a handsome pill box depicting horse riding in a landscape and other bucolic scenes.

THE WILLOW TEAROOMS

CATHERINE (KATE) CRANSTON PIONEERED THE POPU-
LARITY OF THE TEAROOM IN GLASGOW DURING THE
late nineteenth and early twentieth centuries. When she commissioned
Charles Rennie Mackintosh to decorate the walls of her new tearooms, he
was a young draftsman with the Glasgow architectural firm of Honeyman
& Keppie. Mackintosh had many talents—he not only designed the
interiors of Cranston's tearooms, he also designed the furniture; most
famously, the tall-backed chair that became his signature. Glasgow Style,

the flowering of art and design
that occurred at the end of the
nineteenth century, is now indel-
ibly associated with Mackintosh.
Later, he would become famous
for designing the historic Glasgow
School of Art on Renfrew Street
that would cement his reputation
as a great innovator.

Mackintosh's first commission
for Miss Cranston was to design
the murals at the now defunct
Buchanan Street Tearooms at
91–93 Buchanan Street. Other
tearoom commissions followed:
the Argyle Street Tearooms, the

White Dining Room at the Ingram Street Tearooms in the city center, and, finally, in 1903, both the interior and exterior of the original Willow Tearooms at 217 Sauchiehall Street. The most extravagant of the rooms at the Willow was the Room de Luxe. To enter, customers walked through a set of double doors decorated with leaded glass that revealed a color scheme of grey, purple, and white. In 1911 he returned to Ingram Street to create the Chinese Room, which featured vertical, lattice-style screens. The room was painted a vivid blue while the chairs and bench seating were also upholstered in blue (for this reason, it was nicknamed The Blue Room). Mackintosh also designed the tearooms' spoons and even the waitresses' uniforms.

After being shuttered for many years, the Willow Tearooms reopened in 1983 and the Room de Luxe was restored to its original state. In July 1997, another branch of the Willow Tearooms opened, at 97 Buchanan Street, next door to Kate Cranston's original Buchanan Street Tearooms. It contains restorations of the White Dining Room on the first floor and the Chinese Blue Room on the second, both from the Ingram Street location.

Tea and light meals are served at both the Sauchiehall and Buchanan Street locations. The staff whisk around the room in their black uniforms adorned with white aprons, white trim on their sleeves. One gets the impression that Miss Cranston would approve. A two- or three-course lunch is served. Breakfast and afternoon tea are available all day.

Both tearooms share the same menu but the Buchanan Street location also offers a Willow Champagne afternoon tea (Monday–Saturday from 11am, Sunday 12:30–2:30pm) for £18.45 per person. Champagne comes by the glass (£6.50) or bottle (£35).

THE WILLOW TEAROOM SHOP &
HENDERSON THE JEWELLERS

217 SAUCHIEHALL STREET

☎ (0141 332 0521) · *www.willowtearooms.co.uk*

AND 97 BUCHANAN STREET · ☎ (0141 204 5242)

MON–SAT 9AM–5PM, SUN 11AM–4:15PM

BUCHANAN STREET LOCATION SUN UNTIL 5PM

BOTH THE SAUCHIEHALL AND BUCHANAN STREET TEAROOMS SELL CHARLES RENNIE MACKINTOSH-INSPIRED GIFTS, including kitchen accessories, Glasgow Willow pattern aprons, Willow tea towels, bone china, teas, and postcards. A recreation of the Willow Tearooms menu cover that was originally designed by Mackintosh's wife, Margaret Macdonald, is also for sale.

The Room de Luxe on Sauchiehall Street overlooks Henderson the Jewellers (0141 331 2569), a fourth-generation family-run business that sells Mackintosh-inspired crafts. The Mackintosh Collection, for example, consists of CRM-inspired lead crystal glasses designed exclusively by Glencairn Crystal Studio for Henderson. The shop also carries Mackintosh-style picture frames, Mackintosh-style pewter frames, a CRM-style clock with rose motif, CRM placemats and coasters, and even CRM mouse pads.

WALK 7 ✦ FOOD & DRINK

DAVID SLOAN'S ARCADE CAFÉ

62 Argyll Arcade, 108 Argyle Street ☎ (0141) 221 8886
Noon-10pm · Bar, bistro, and restaurant

Old-fashioned doors serve as an impressive entryway to "Glasgow's oldest bar and restaurant." Look for the lovely tile and mosaic of flowers and pillars as you walk up a flight of stairs to the main entrance. The original architectural features of this structure (erected circa 1797) remain intact: vaulted ceiling, marble fireplace, and stained glass windows. On the second floor is a grand ballroom, cozy snugs lend an intimate atmosphere, and the wooden grand bar is gorgeous. The menu is eclectic and may include spinach and ricotta ravioli with pine nuts and sage butter (at £6.95), as well as sandwiches and salads. A tour of the building can be arranged at 0131 221 8886.

GRAND FISH AND CHIPS

Italian Centre, 17 John Street ☎ (0141)552 40`7
Lunch & pre-theatre dinner, dinner · Moderate

Despite its name, Grand Fish and Chips offers more than just fish and chips. It serves plenty of other seafood dishes, including monkfish, haddock, sole, cod, mussels, and prawns. Spread out over two levels—the bar and restaurant are on the mezzanine level, the glass conservatory at the rear of the restaurant—it has outdoor dining, Italian style, in good weather. On Mondays–Thursdays from 5–7 pm, a two-course meal costs £10.95, three courses, £12.95.

WALK 8 ✦ MERCHANT CITY

HITHERTO

14/1 INGRAM STREET

☎ (0141) 552 5693 · *www.hithertoshop.co.uk*

SUN–WED, FRI 11AM–6PM, THUR 11AM–7PM, SAT 10AM–6PM

THERE'S QUIRKY AND THEN THERE'S QUIRKY. HITHERTO FALLS INTO THE LATTER CATEGORY. BUT OTHER WORDS can also apply: eclectic or, perhaps, eccentric. It is both fair and accurate to say that Hitherto carries items that no one else does. Quite a lot of what you see here is the work of students and/or graduates of the famous Glasgow School of Art (GSA), which also accounts for the mellow mood of the place. And is it sheer coincidence that the McIntyre Hogg Building that houses Hitherto has historic connections to GSA itself? A marker outside reads, "On the 6th January 1845, the Glasgow School of Art opened on this site where it remained until 1869, before moving to The Corporation Galleries in Sauchiehall Street and finally the Charles Rennie Mackintosh Building in Renfrew Street in 1899."

Hitherto is a boutique within a coffeehouse. You will need to walk through the Tinderbox café next door since Hitherto is tucked away in the back. Hitherto sells items from around the world but owner Krista Blake also believes in promoting the work of local talent. As Blake mentions, everything

changes. What you see today you will not necessarily see tomorrow or, for that matter, ever again. Indeed, Blake oftentimes commissions local artists to design one-of-a-kind t-shirts, which change every few months.

Cozy leather chairs and sofas encourage customers to linger. Many from the adjacent Tinderbox often bring their cup of coffee to the shop and just hang out. Huddled away in a corner of the room is the travel equipment and gear of the Glasgow rock band Teenage Fan Club (Krista is married to Norman Blake, the founder of the band, something that she tries to downplay). Hitherto is more than a quirky shop, though. Blake also sponsors workshops, exhibitions, record and book release parties, storytelling sessions, classes and craft workshops in knitting, sewing, embroidery, crocheting, and fabric painting, and even free gigs by local bands.

JONATHAN AVERY

SHERIFF COURT BUILDING, 80 HUTCHESON STREET

☎ (0141) 552 1000 · *www.jonathanavery.co.uk*

MON–FRI 9:30AM–5:30PM, SAT 10AM–5:30PM

L IGHT AND AIRY, SPACIOUS, AND FULL OF LOVELY THINGS, JONATHAN AVERY IS A FAMILY BUSINESS THAT SPECIALIZES in home products, including handmade and hand painted furniture made at workshops in the Scottish Borders. The shop carries houseware items from numerous UK companies, such as teapots from Emma Bridgewater, fabrics and wallpaper from Jane Churchill, and glassware

from Parlane. The shop also sells smaller items such as birdhouses, quilts, and cookware accessories. The Glasgow shop is located in a handsome Greek Revival structure erected in 1842 that once served as the city's municipal and county building.

WALK 8 ✦ FOOD & DRINK

TINDERBOX

14 Ingram Street ☎ (0141) 552 6907
Mon-Sat 7:15am-10pm, Sun 7:45am-10pm
Breakfast, lunch, & dinner · Inexpensive

Tinderbox is an espresso bar, a breakfast stop (try the muesli with milk and organic cherries in syrup or the purple power porridge, organic porridge with organic wild blueberries in syrup), or a good place for lunch and a light meal. Tinderbox also serves soups, pie, hot and cold sandwiches, tea, Italian soda, wine, beer, and cider as well as cakes and various sweets.

CRANBERRY'S TEAROOM & FINE GIFTS

30 Wilson Street ☎ (0141) 552 3676
Mon-Sat 9am-5:30pm, Sun 10am-5pm, Breakfast & lunch · Inexpensive

This Merchant City tearoom and espresso bar serves various light fare such as toasties, paninis, wraps, bagels, and sandwiches (one with tasty Loch Fyne smoked salmon), lasagna, and haggis in a mellow atmosphere. Wine and beer are also available. Under the glass counter you'll see plenty of mouthwatering sweets.

THE CITY MERCHANT

97 Candleriggs ☎ (0141) 553 1577
Mon-Sat Noon-10:30pm, Lunch & dinner · Expensive

Considered one of the finest restaurants in Glasgow, the City Merchant serves both Scottish and Italian food. Typical starters might be a haggis, wild mushroom, and Lochaber smoked-cheese tartlet or oysters from the West Coast. Main entrées might include a Scottish seafood platter, Shetland salmon, monkfish, whole Scottish lobster, or prime Scots steak. The "Scotalia" menu, at £19.95, is available from noon–2:30pm and from 5–10:30pm Monday–Thursday and from noon–5pm Friday and Saturday. The desserts too are special, such as the cranachan ice cream, a traditional clootie dumpling ("a mixture of flour, spices, and raisins boiled in a cloth for four hours") or baked cranachan Alaska. Entrées average between £15.95–22.

CAFÉ GANDOLFI

64 Albion Street ☎ (0141) 552 6813
Mon-Sat 9am-11:30pm, Sun Noon-11:30pm · Moderate

Café Gandolfi has a rustic look, with wooden furniture designed by the late Glasgow School of Art graduate Tim Stead, and emphasizes fresh Scottish produce, including black pudding from Macleod and Macleod of Stornoway or smoked venison from the Rannoch Smokery on Rannoch Moor. The café also serves light meals, salads, sandwiches, and pasta. In June 2007, the owners opened Gandolfi Fish (0141 552 9475; Monday–Sunday Noon–2:30pm, 5:30–10:30pm; 84 Albion Street), which, as its name indicates, specializes in fish dishes such as Scottish seafood broth, scallops with parsley and tomato risotto, grilled half lobster, or whole baked mackerel.

BABBITY BOWSTER

16-18 Blackfriars Street ☎ (0141) 552 5055
Lunch & dinner · Inexpensive

Named after a traditional Scottish country dance, this all-purpose cheery pub, café, and restaurant (it also functions as an affordable inn) is a wonderful place for a meal or just a pint. The décor is soothing: dark brown wooden tables and white walls, beams painted with colorful stylized flowers, comfy benches with soft cushions. There's also an outdoor patio. Don't forget to admire the pub's namesake plaque above the fireplace: a kilted Scotsman doing a wee jig with two dancing figures and a piper. Upstairs is the more upscale Schottische (0141 552 7774), which serves sophisticated Scots cuisine.

GLASGOW STREET MARKETS

THE BARRAS

Gallowgate ☎ (0141) 552 4601

Sat-Sun 10am-5pm

Aₙ OPEN-AIR STREET MARKET LOCATED BETWEEN THE GALLOWGATE AND LONDON ROAD IN GLASGOW'S EAST End, the Barras sells antiques, bric-a-brac, clothing, food, woolens, kilts, and jewelry. But, truth be told, one has the feeling almost anything can be bought and sold here. Because stalls are rented on a week-to-week basis, customers are always in for a surprise. Beginning at 8am on the last Saturday of each month, the Barras sponsors a Farmers Market at the courtyard of the Barras Centre between Moncur and Stevenston streets. On sale are organic fruits and vegetables, meat, smoked trout and salmon, smoked cheeses, and such unusual items as ostrich meat and wild boar.

"Barra" is a Glaswegian term for barrow. The history of this market begins with one woman, Margaret Russell, who, in 1923, saved up enough money to open a small fruit shop in the Bridgeton neighborhood in Glasgow's East

End. Together with her future husband, James McIvor, the couple set up a business, renting out horses and carts to traders who hawked their wares around the wealthier areas of Glasgow. Eventually, they were able to rent out barrows to traders, establishing Saturday morning as their trading time. Today, it remains a place to experience a bit of "local color."

PADDY'S MARKET
Shipbank Lane · Open Daily

Also in the East End, Paddy's Market has sold secondhand clothes and more for 200 years. Started in the nineteenth century by Irish immigrants—many of them fleeing the Irish Famine—it was given the sobriquet of "Paddy's" market. It has moved several times over the years, but since 1935, it has been located in Shipbank Lane. Buyers beware: Admittedly a bit rough round the edges, in recent years there has been talk of shutting it down because of concerns over crime and counterfeit items. Still, in addition to the Barras mentioned above, this flea market offers some of the best chances for visitors to hear the irrepressible Glasgow "patter" at its most animated.

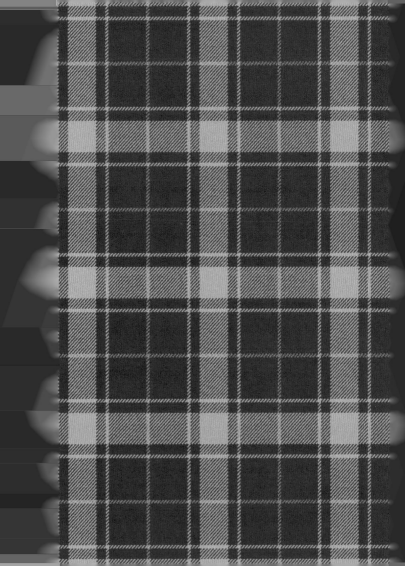

WALK 9 ✦ GREAT WESTERN ROAD

TIMOROUS BEASTIES

384 GREAT WESTERN ROAD

☎ (0141) 337 2622 · *www.timorousbeasties.com*

MON–THURS, SAT 10:30AM–6PM;

FRI 10:30AM–5PM; SUN 12:30–5PM

THE NAME OF THIS DESIGN SHOP COMES FROM ROBERT BURNS'S 1785 POEM, "TO A MOUSE"

> Wee, sleekit, cowrin tim'rous beastie,
>
> O, what a panic's in thy breastie!
>
> Thou need na start awa sae hasty
>
> Wi' bickering brattle!

Founded in 1990 by Alistair McAuley and Paul Simmons, Timorous Beasties is known for its surreal and subversive textiles and wallpapers: think graphic novels (à la Frank Miller's *Sin City*) meets urban art meets creepy-crawlie imagery. McAuley and Simmons's style is often referred to as Glasgow Toile. Typically, it consists of a pastoral scene—but not at Timorous Beasties. On the contrary, McAuley and Simmons's visions are often quite nightmarish, populated by

crack addicts, prostitutes, and homeless men and women. One critic once described their style as "William Morris on acid." Clearly, the designs are not to everyone's taste. But those folk with an adventurous and macabre sense of humor will probably appreciate it.

McAuley and Simmons met at the Glasgow School of Art. They started out designing fabrics and wallpaper for private clients before opening their own shop in 2004. By introducing black humor into designs that are typically idyllic, McAuley and Simmons insert a bit of controversy. Their designs are deliberately confrontational. "Our subversive creativity comes from pure self-indulgence," says McAuley. "Our work is based on this is what I like. We don't conform to any kind of market."

The beasties in McAuley and Simmon's designs are hardly timorous, either. Lampshades are decorated with iguanas and flies; a gossamer lace comes with a devil's face.

CALEDONIA BOOKS

483 GREAT WESTERN ROAD

☎ (0141) 334-9663 · *www.caledoniabooks.co.uk*

MON–SAT 10:30AM–6PM

THIS SECONDHAND AND ANTIQUARIAN BOOKSHOP, LOCATED ON A BUSY STRETCH OF GREAT WESTERN ROAD, CONSISTS of two large rooms and an attic overflowing with books on many topics, including literary criticism, military, biography, travel, art, theater, drama, film, media, philosophy, literature, and poetry. There is also a large Scottish section covering Scots poetry, history, and literature. Caledonia Books is an old-fashioned bookshop. The atmosphere here is mellow, the staff helpful as customers quietly peruse the shelves while classical music plays softly in the background.

WATERMELON

603 GREAT WESTERN ROAD

☎ (0141) 334 3900

MON–SAT 11AM–6PM, SUN NOON–6PM

GAVIN O'BRIEN USED TO WORK FOR A WHOLESALE FIRM THAT SUPPLIED VINTAGE CLOTHING TO ARMSTRONG'S (see p. 40). Now he has a vintage shop of his own. The black storefront with a red door is a dramatic entranceway into a place that specializes in male and female clothing from the 1940s to the 1980s. The atmosphere is funky and laid back. Members of the Glasgow-based indie band, Belle and Sebastian, are said to be fans of the shop. It has an ambiance that skews towards the quirky: a Raleigh chopper bike hangs by chains from the ceiling; dresses on hangers dangle from beams; American and Confederate flags decorate the walls. O'Brien has a selection of leather jackets, tops, jumpers, hats, purses, boots, shoes, kilts and waistcoats. Variously colored ties (at £4 each) are draped across the bottom half of the front door. The effect is playfully good-natured.

COLLEGE OF PIPING SHOP

16–24 OTAGO STREET

☎ (0141) 342 5252 · *www.college-of-piping.co.uk*

THE COLLEGE OF PIPING LIES UNOBTRUSIVELY OFF BUSY GREAT WESTERN ROAD. IT'S UNLIKELY YOU'LL stumble across it by accident. More often than not, people come here with a purpose in mind. Its size is deceiving—this nonprofit organization also operates a school, a shop, and a museum and publishes a magazine, *Piping Times*.

The shop is tiny, the museum cramped but full of fascinating information, a must for anyone with an interest in Scotland's national instrument. Established in 1944, the museum started out in an old whisky warehouse; today it is housed in a modern building that is the only building in the world

designed specifically for the teaching of the great Highland bagpipe.

The shop stocks bagpipes and bagpipe accessories such as practice chanters, reeds, pipe bags, pipe cases, mouthpieces and blow-sticks, tuners and metronomes. Also for sale are sheet music, music books, music scores, and piping CDs as well as kilts and Highland dress wear (including jackets, sporrans, waistcoats, ghillie brogues), tutor books and CDs, and pipe starter kits. Each kit comes with a practice chanter with reed and a tutoring CD-ROM.

THE NORTHERN MEETING, INVERNESS

PIPING COMPETITIONS

WILL BE HELD IN THE

NORTHERN MEETING ROOMS

CHURCH STREET, INVERNESS, ON

WEDNESDAY AND THURSDAY

24TH & 25TH SEPTEMBER, 1958

COMMENCING AT 9.30 A.M. EACH DAY

PRIZES.

			1st Prize.	2nd Prize.	3rd Prize.	4th Prize.	5th Prize.
WEDNESDAY.							
A.	PIOBAIREACHD—Gold Medal Competition	Gold Medal presented by the Highland Society of London and	£10	£7	£5	£3	£2
B.	MARCHES . . .		£5		£4	£3	-	-
C.	MARCH, STRATHSPEY & REEL— Silver Star Competition	Silver Star presented by the Royal Scottish Pipers' Society and	£10		£6	£4	-	-
	JUNIOR COMPETITION for Boys under 18 years of age . (GIFT TOKEN)	Chanter presented by Royal Scottish Pipers' Society and	£2	£1 10s	£1	10s	-
	(Confined to Counties of Caithness, Sutherland, Inverness, Ross and Cromarty, Nairn, Moray and Banff)							
	THURSDAY.							
D.	PIOBAIREACHD—Open and Clasp and MacBrayne's Centenary Challenge Cup Competition	MacBrayne's Centenary Challenge Cup presented by David MacBraynes Limited. Clasp presented by Northern Meeting and	£10		£7	£5	£3	£2
E.	STRATHSPEY & REEL . .		£5		£4	£3	-	-
F.	JIGS . . .		£5		£4	£3	-	-

The 1st and 5th money prizes for Competition "A" and 1st and 3rd money prizes for Competition "D" are presented by the Piobaireach Society. All other money prizes presented by the Northern Meeting. In addition a payment of £1 5s will be made to Competitors for expenses (exclusive of Competitors in Junior Competition). For conditions see Entry Forms. *Women and Girls are not eligible to compete in any event.*

ENTRIES CLOSE ON 13th SEPTEMBER 1958. NO ENTRY FEE.

Entry Forms with fuller rules and details from JAMES SOUTH, Secretary, 8 Ardross Terrace Inverness, and from all the Bagpipe Makers Shops.

VOLTAIRE & ROUSSEAU

12-14 OTAGO LANE

☎ (0141) 339 1811 · NO CREDIT CARDS

MON–SAT 11AM–6:30PM

THE NAME ITSELF INDICATES THAT THIS IS A BOOKSHOP FOR SERIOUS READERS. IT IS NOT EASY TO FIND, BUT off Great Western Road, down a cobblestone lane, there it stands, its name painted on an old, weathered sign. Voltaire & Rousseau is a ramshackle kind of second-hand bookstore; the word "cluttered" doesn't quite do it justice. Books are everywhere—on the shelves, often haphazardly, and scattered on the floor. Its strong suits are Scottish titles, literature, and history. Fantasy books are also plentiful. A portrait of Robert Burns, a great reader and self-taught scholar, hangs above the front desk, watching over customers who roam the aisles. All books in the front room can be had for £1. You'll never know what you'll find here, and that's a part of the shop's roughhewn charm.

WALK 9 FOOD & DRINK

STRAVAIGIN

28 Gibson Street ☎ (0141) 334 2665
Noon-11pm Daily · Expensive

Off Great Western Road, this mainstay of the upscale Glasgow restaurant scene specializing in Scottish cuisine doesn't disappoint. It may be on the pricey side, but it is one of the best restaurants in Glasgow. (See also page 172.)

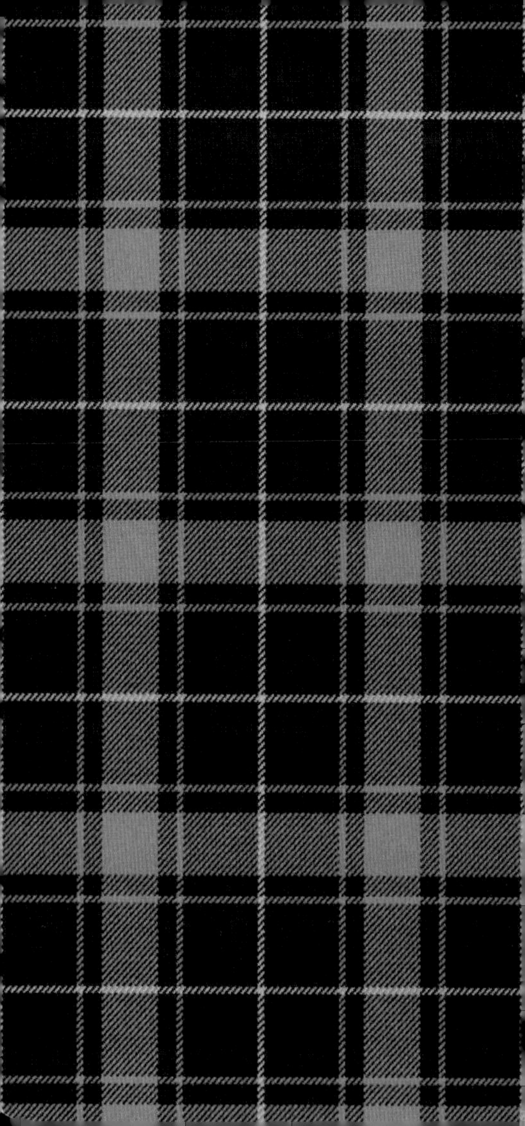

WALK 10 ✦ BYRES ROAD

BELONG

114 BYRES ROAD

☎ (0141) 576 5076 · *www.belong-jewellry.co.uk*

MON–SAT 10AM–6PM, SUN NOON–5PM

BELONG SPECIALIZES IN DESIGNER JEWELRY, MOSTLY FROM THE UNITED KINGDOM. (ITS NAME IS A PLAY ON the music hall standard "I Belong to Glasgow," the city's unofficial

theme song.) "All our wooden jewelry is turned by hand," explains the manager. Owner Dawn Forest, he says, sources the jewelry and non-jewelry items from the UK as well as throughout the world.

Belong stocks brooches, rings, earrings, and bangles, as well as necklaces (such as freshwater pearl or amethyst) and bracelets (including silver and black onyx, Swarovski crystal, and sterling silver). Belong also carries a few non-jewelry items such as handwoven silk scarves.

THE SENTRY BOX

175 GREAT GEORGE STREET (OFF BYRES ROAD)

☎ (0141) 334 6070

MON–FRI 9:30AM–5:30PM, SUN 1PM–5PM

THE SENTRY BOX HAS BEEN A SCOTTISH FIXTURE FOR THIRTY YEARS OR SO. AN OLD-FASHIONED TOY SHOP, IT is cozy and usually crammed with families and their children, often from the surrounding West End and University of Glasgow neighborhood. Children adore the shop's finger puppets, wooden toys, kites and mobiles,

jigsaws and toy animals. The rocking horses recall the childhoods of another era. Also, on hand are coloring books as well as various educational toys, games, and puzzles. It offers a gift wrapping service and some lovely cards. A traditional shop in the best sense of the word.

THE NANCY SMILLIE SHOP

53 CRESSWELL STREET

☎ (0141) 334 4240 · *www.nancysmillieshop.com*

MON–FRI 10AM–5:30PM, SAT 10AM–6PM, SUN NOON–5PM

THE SIGN SAYS IT ALL: "ECLECTIC IS THE WORD." ECLECTIC IT MAY BE BUT EVERYTHING IN THE SHOP CONSISTS OF individually or handcrafted items. Owner Nancy Smillie sources furniture from throughout the world. Smillie also carries original artwork and prints from artists both local and interna-

tional. An artist herself (she was trained as a potter), Smillie's business philosophy—and it really can apply to her life as well—believes in juxtaposing a product that some might consider silly or trivial and setting it next to an exquisite work of art. In other words, it all comes down to serendipity. Whether in her shop or out on the street, life is full of delightfully random encounters.

Smillie stocks big item products (tables and chairs, sofas and beds and such) but also smaller objects (jewelry, necklaces, bracelets, handmade felt bags, candles). She especially appreciates the work of quirky artists with their own peculiar take on the world such as the whimsical cherry wood handmade clocks of Brighton artist David Booker or the hand painted

ceramics of Bryony Burn, another UK artist. At her shop you may also find handcrafted chess sets, handcrafted mirrors that use recycled newspapers, or whatever else captures her fancy.

For anyone who wants a souvenir of Glasgow's West End, be sure to pick up one of the collection of giclee prints (if available) that celebrate life in this most exquisite of neighborhoods (giclee prints are known for their archival quality inks and better color accuracy). The prints include "West End Shopping," "West End Living," and "Ashton Lane."

THE INDEPENDENT SHOPS
OF RUTHVEN MEWS

DOWN THE COBBLESTONE LANES OFF BYRES ROAD AND OPPOSITE THE HILLHEAD UNDERGROUND, THE DISTINC-tive shops of Ruthven Mews consist mostly of a series of independent local businesses, many of them housed in low-slung, small buildings. It is worth a stroll not only to soak up the atmosphere but also just to appreciate the hard work of these small business owners who are trying to survive in a world of large chains.

Relics is a fascinating collector's shop—chaotic best sums it up—that sells antiques, used books, golf bags, old photographs of Glasgow, and various bric-a-brac, even old typewriters and old guitars as well as a large collection of recordings from easy listening to jazz to pop and punk. Zico (named after the Brazilian soccer player) is a retro sports and fashion shop specializing in soccer memorabilia and women's designer wear.

Glorious Clothing offers quality secondhand clothing plus bags, shoes, scarves, jewelry, and vintage clothing. Circa Vintage sells hand-picked vintage clothes, accessories, jewelry, handbags, dresses, hats, costume jewelry, leather jackets, and all kinds of coats, especially from the 1930s up to the 1980s, and a woolen suit that would do Jackie Kennedy proud. Finally, The Glory Hole, another vintage shop, has a nice collection of secondhand clothes, bags, and shoes.

STARRY STARRY NIGHT

21 DOWANSIDE LANE

☎ (0141) 334 4778 (BETHSY GRAY) AND

(0141) 337 1837 (VINTAGE SHOP)

MON–SAT 10AM–5:30PM

THE EXTERIOR IS PAINTED A DARK GREEN. FLOWER POTS HANG OUTSIDE UNDER A GREEN-AND-WHITE-STRIPED awning. Inside, in the back of the shop, Bethsy Gray works diligently, oblivious to the outside world until, that is, a customer interrupts her with a question or a comment. Only then will she stop what she's doing and gladly engage in conversation. Trained in Denmark, Bethsy specializes in handmade silver jewelry, with insets of opals, moonstones, or garnets, for example. Her jewelry is simple but stylish.

Bethsy shares the space with a vintage shop that specializes in a wonderful and unpredictable—not to mention affordable—collection of retro items from lacy to tweedy clothing to cardigans to frocks, including Victorian-era gowns, cocktail dresses from the 1920s and 1930s, and garments from the 1970s, as well as accessories.

WALK 10 ✦ FOOD & DRINK

ÒRAN MÓR

Top of Byres Road ☎ (0141) 357 6200
Breakfast, lunch, & dinner · Moderate

Òran Mór (Gaelic for "big song") offers an unusual combination of food and eclectic diversions. Housed in a former church, the physical space includes two bars, two restaurants, and a nightclub. Breakfast, lunch, and dinner are available with most items averaging between £5.95 to just under £8 (dinner prices are slightly higher). Along with your meal, you'll experience some fine entertainment. "A Pie, a Play and a Pint" presents hour-long plays, usually by Scottish, Irish, and English playwrights for £10, which includes the cost of a pie (steak or otherwise) and a drink; "A Dinner, a Drama and a Dram," at £25, includes a short play and a two-course dinner, coffee, and a wee dram; while "A Concert, a Cocktail and a Canapé," also £10, includes the concert, drinks, and canapés. Whichever you choose, it is a unique experience and well worth it.

KEMBER & JONES

134 Byres Road ☎ (0141) 337 3851
Daily and every evening except Sunday
Breakfast, lunch, & dinner · Inexpensive

Kember refers to Phil Kember from Portsmouth; Jones to Claire Jones from Glasgow. Now considered somewhat of a West End institution, Kember & Jones is a delightful deli and café as well as a kitchenware and cookbook store. But it is especially known for its home-baked cakes and pastries such as the scrumptious pistachio, cardamom, and orange tart. The café also serves some forty types of meringues as well as tartlets with a variety of fillings. It's good for an early breakfast (such as homemade granola with berries and yogurt or pancakes with ricotta and honeycomb) or lunchtime snack and/or pre-dinner meal. Wine too.

STRAVAIGIN 2

8 Ruthven Lane ☎ (0141) 334 7165
Lunch & dinner, closed Monday · Moderate

Think global, eat local is the motto of this wonderful West End restaurant set in a handsome white stucco building with black trim. The menu is eclectic, combining Scottish produce with exotic touches. The burgers are cooked using a thirty-year-old recipe and range in size from 6 oz. to 12 oz. to a massive 18 oz. Choose between beef, Thai chicken, or wild boar. Friendly service. Also at 28 Gibson Street, ☎ (0141) 334 2665.

THE BOTHY RESTAURANT

11 Ruthven Lane ☎ (0141) 334 4040
Daily noon to 10pm · Moderate

Modern classics with a touch of the traditional—from the barn-like setting ("bothy" is a Scots term for barn or shelter) to the kilted staff. The Bothy serves soups, tuna melt sandwiches, and focaccia. The "braw deal" set menu consists of two courses for £9.95 or three courses for £12.95. The Sunday Roast ranges in price from £11.95 to £13.95 and is available from noon to 6PM. Dinner items could start with a bowl of cullen skink (a traditional Scots soup usually consisting of finnan haddock, onion, milk, potatoes, and butter) with toasted oats and a piece of crusty bread, followed by Grampian chicken over roasted rump of Perthshire lamb, West Coast scallops, Scottish filet steak, or pan-seared king scallops accompanied by a black pudding potato cake.

THE UBIQUITOUS CHIP

12 Ashton Lane ☎ (0141) 334 5007
Lunch & dinner · Expensive

Winner of numerous best city restaurant in Scotland awards, the Chip, as it's known, is considered one of the finest restaurants in Scotland. It's been around a long time—since 1973—and yet it never sits on its laurels. Typical lunch starters could be venison or vegetarian haggis with turnip cream or Dumfriesshire rabbit, pear and pistachio sausage with carrot and coriander salad. Main courses might be Orkney organic salmon, mallard duck confit, or Mallaig skate wings. All of this great food comes at a price. Although the main restaurant is expensive, the brasserie lunch menu is more affordable. Sunday lunch, which includes an appetizer, costs £18.65 per person. Failing that, there's always bar food that averages £4–5 per item.

ALSO WORTH A VISIT

Edinburgh

....

CORNICHE

2 Jeffrey Street ☎ (0131) 556 3707

Since it opened more than thirty years ago, Nina Grant's fashion boutique for men and women has been a beloved fixture on the Edinburgh scene. Corniche was the first boutique to bring the English designer Betty Jackson to the attention of Scottish shoppers. But Grant also supports local designers too; names to look for are Holly and Jackie Burke and Cecile Paul.

FRONTIERS

254 Canongate ☎ (0131) 556 2791

Also at 16 Stafford Street (0131) 476 3449

This independent boutique carries UK and European labels as well as owner Jane Forbes's own label. Frontiers carries slacks and tops from the Saltwater label; scarves by Ingrid Tait, who runs Tait & Style from her native Orkney; woven fabrics and woolens of the Galashiels-based Eribé; and purses by Sophie Williams and Kate Sheridan.

RENE WALRUS

30 St. Mary's Street ☎ (0131) 558 8120

www.renewalrus.co.uk

In addition to owner Janet McCrorie's own range, this boutique sells designer jewelry, specializing in wedding accessories and custom pieces. Tiaras can be custom made.

PAM JENKINS

41 Thistle Street ☎ (0131) 225 3242

www.pamjenkins.co.uk

All the big names are represented at this small and stylish shoe store, including Jimmy Choo, Rupert Sanderson, Chloe, Kate Spade, Patrick Cox, and Marc Jacobs, along with the largest range of Christian Louboutin shoes and bags in Scotland and the north of England.

LINZI CRAWFORD

27 Dublin Street ☎ (0131) 558 7558

www.linzicrawford.com

A women's clothing shop, Linzi Crawford offers the largest collection in Edinburgh of such labels as Paule Vasseur, Claudia Stevens, Michel Ambers, Joseph Ribkoff, Alain Manoukian, and Linea Raffaelli as well as shoes by Lisa Kay, hats by Nigel Rayment and by Yvette Jeffs and jewelry by Barbara Easton. The diverse and eclectic collection emphasizes special occasion wear, eveningwear, and casual wear.

MIAM MIAM

125 Bruntsfield Place ☎ (0131) 221 0037

www.miam.miam-co.uk

A cheery boutique—stylish and chic but without any pretense—run by a former can-can dancer from the Moulin Rouge. Miam Miam (the name means "yum yum" in French) specializes in French antique and contemporary home furnishings.

Glasgow

....

FELIX AND OSCAR

459 Great Western Road ☎ (0141) 339 8585

www.felixandoscar.co.uk

Trendy lifestyle shop Felix and Oscar sells contemporary accessories for women such as handbags and shoulder bags and items for men (a men's cologne, for example, inspired by the Isle of Skye) as well as an extensive collection of children's clothing. Also on display here are witty gifts, jewelry, mugs and cards, and various lifestyle books—on cooking, humor, and cocktails.

FLOUNCE

493 Great Western Road ☎ (0141) 339 1011

Lovely shop in Glasgow's leafy West End that specializes in curtains, cushions, and accessories.

AUTHOR'S FAVORITES

SHOPS BY SPECIALTY

ALPHABETICAL INDEX

Glasgow

SHOPS

PUBS, CAFES & RESTAURANTS

NOTES

NOTES

NOTES

NOTES

NOTES

NOTES

NOTES

ACKNOWLEDGMENTS

Additional reporting was done by Liz Small in Glasgow and Su Clark in Edinburgh. Thank you! The author also wishes to thank Erlend and Hélène Clouston and Diane and Robert Rae for their gracious hospitality. Dorothy Wordsworth's quote about Edinburgh's White Hart Inn is taken from *Recollections of a Tour Made in Scotland* edited by Carol Kyros Walker (1997). In addition, I would not have been able to write the book without the generosity of my cousins in Glasgow: Janet, Bert, Elaine, and Lesley McFarlane. Additional thanks are extended to Eileen Macdonald, a Highlander living in the Lowlands, and to my editor Angela Hederman at The Little Bookroom, and, of course, to all the merchants, for their time, cooperation, and patience.

ABOUT THE AUTHOR

Born in Glasgow, Scotland, JUNE SKINNER SAWYERS has written and lectured extensively on Scotland. Her father, a carpenter, used to run his own carpentry business on Charlotte Street in the heart of Glasgow; her mother used to work at Gray, Dunn's, the famous biscuit factory, also in Glasgow. She has written or edited eighteen books, many with a Scottish or Celtic theme, including *Maverick Guide to Scotland*, *The Scottish Bed & Breakfast Book*, *Celtic Music*, *The Road North: 300 Years of Classic Scottish Travel Writing*, and *Dreams of Elsewhere: The Selected Travel Writings of Robert Louis Stevenson*. She writes a travel book column, "The Resourceful Traveler," for the *Chicago Tribune*.

ABOUT THE PHOTOGRAPHERS

ALEX HEWITT has worked as a photographer and picture editor in Edinburgh and other parts of Scotland for the past ten years. Currently he is a Picture Editor at *The Scotsman* and co-runs Writer Pictures, a boutique literary portraiture library.

SUSIE LOWE is an award-winning photographer based in Edinburgh. She works for a diverse range of clients, specializing in interiors, portraiture and fashion. Susie's work is regularly featured in leading style magazines in Scotland.